Develop and Market YOUR CREATIVE IDEAS

2nd Edition

Dale A. Davis

Edited by Vickie Reierson

OASIS PRESS

The Oasis Press® / PSI Research
Grants Pass, Oregon

092596

Published by The Oasis Press®

Editor: Vickie Reierson
Editorial Assistance: Sean P. Murray and Linda Pinkham
Book Design and Typography: Constance C. Dickinson
Typographic Assistance: Jan Olsson and Linda Pinkham
Cover Design: Steven Burns and Constance C. Dickinson

Please direct any comments, questions, or suggestions regarding this book to The Oasis Press®/ PSI Research:

Editorial Department
300 North Valley Drive
Grants Pass, OR 97526
(541) 479-9464

The Oasis Press® is a Registered Trademark of Publishing Services, Inc., an Oregon corporation doing business as PSI Research.

Library of Congress Cataloging-in-Publication Data

Davis, Dale A. (Dale Allen)
Develop and market your creative ideas / Dale A. Davis ; edited by Vickie Reierson. -- 2nd ed.
p. cm. -- (PSI successful business library)
Rev. ed. of: How to develop & market creative business ideas. 1st ed. c1991.
Includes bibliographical references and index.
ISBN 1-55571-383-1
1. New products--Marketing. I. Davis, Dale A. (Dale Allen). How to develop & market creative business ideas. II. Title. III. Series.
HF5415.153. D38 1996
658.5'75--dc20 96-8709

Printed in the United States of America
Second edition 10 9 8 7 6 5 4 3 2 1

Printed on recycled paper when available.

To Wendy, my nine-year-old daughter,
a very special young lady
whose imagination and enthusiasm
has allowed me to see the world again —
through the curiosity and wonder of a child's eyes.

The awe and astonishment
that shows in her eyes every day
allows me to see,
without preconceived notions of what can't be done,
that anything is possible and life is endless in its wonder.

It is not the critic who counts,
not the man who points out how the strong man stumbled
or where the doer of deeds could have done them better.
The credit belongs to the man who is actually in the arena;
whose face is marred by dust and sweat and blood;
who strives valiantly;
who errs and comes short again and again;
who knows the great enthusiasms,
the great devotions,
and spends himself in a worthy cause;
who, at best, knows the triumph of high achievement,
and who, at the worst, if he fails,
at least fails while daring greatly,
so that his place shall never be
with those cold and timid souls
who know neither victory nor defeat.

Theodore Roosevelt
April 23, 1917

Ode to an Inventor

You have an idea and must give it a try,
    You have a need to create and see your concepts fly;
You work out the bugs and create a little joy,
    You act like a kid with a brand new toy;
You try every option and use every trick,
    You are determined and won't be licked;
You know this business is not easy, and wonder why you dare,
    You, my friend, are an inventor, so let the world beware.

Dale A. Davis

Table of Contents

Foreword

From the earliest days of my career as an automobile designer at General Motors, I saw corporate staff experts in each of the various professions of engineering, marketing analysis, economics, patent law, consumer research, wholesale and retail level distribution, assembled to accomplish the task of bringing a designer's idea, usually in the form of a sketch, through the developmental stages to reach the reality of the marketplace.

Whether the idea was as simple as the shape of a knob, or as complex as an automobile, the processes and procedures required to determine the feasibility for production and mass marketing were virtually the same. Considerations — such as materials costs; production engineering, which often conflicted with the original design concept; consumer attitude research to assess probable sales potential; legal protection; and patent searches — were as extensive and costly for many details as they were for concepts that constituted major advances in technology.

In private practice, as an industrial designer and a principal of the Design Center of San Francisco, I coordinated the participation of a variety of professionals commissioned by our corporate clients to perform these component duties, and for some clients, we developed teams from our own sources.

Many of our Design Center clients came to us after years of futile efforts attempting to develop an idea or concept to the point of practical design, volume production, packaging and distribution, promotion and mass marketing success.

For the past thirty years, designing new products, developing and implementing marketing plans, and completing market research for Fortune 500 corporations and individual clients has made the processes involved in these activities a matter of daily routine in the practice of industrial design. However, to the inventor or individual entrepreneur, working alone, trying to go through the process for the first time, the conglomeration of procedures and diverse disciplines involved in bringing an inspirational idea to the reality of mass production and volume marketing can be an insurmountable melange.

With each design development project, we gained wider knowledge and experience of the many facets involved in the implementation of an idea or concept. With each new endeavor, we found major differences, but we also found certain principle similarities that were common to virtually all such processes of development.

The primary developmental processes necessary to successfully achieve these Herculean tasks have been captured, distilled, defined, and explained between these covers you now hold in your hand.

Here, for the first time in my experience, my professional associate, Mr. Dale Davis, has put the information needed to guide you through the morass of activities involved in the development of an idea through to a finished product, in a single, easy-to-use reference. By avoiding the use of technical nomenclature or professional jargon, Mr. Davis provides a guide for either the amateur or professional. *Develop and Market Your Creative Ideas* is a practical pathway to reach the goals required to bring your idea to a constructive integration with the real world. It is a must in the library of any serious entrepreneur or inventor, and will always occupy a special place in our industrial design office library for quick and easy referencing.

JERRY CUMBUS
Director, Automotive and
Industrial Design Research Center

Preface

When the first edition of this book was published in 1991, the 90s were just beginning and taking a product or idea to market was exciting and required a commitment like no other. Since then, many changes have taken place. Currently, in 1996, more than 63 million Americans are doing some kind of work from their homes. Because of changing technology and industry trends, the workplace is full of telecommuters, moonlighters, weekend entrepreneurs, "homepreneurs," and independent contract workers.

One of the many reasons for the shift in how business is being conducted is that industry is competing on a different level in a more diverse market. This has forced companies to become more competitive, downsizing and streamlining their operations, thus cutting benefits and reducing wages. According to the *Washington Post* Writer's Group, earnings between 1979 and 1994 fell 28 percent for men who didn't finish high school. Wages fell 16 percent for high school graduates, and 11 percent for those with some college education. During this same time, corporate downsizing increased its demands upon its subcontractors and other out-sourced workers, allowing many workers living on less income to form their own part-time and full-time businesses. Another main contributor to the changes in industry has been advancing technology, which is allowing many entrepreneurs to work out of their virtual offices, utilizing the Internet and telecommuting to their clients.

The bright side to these changes is that most of us like what we are doing. Working from the virtual office is simply another way of working smarter and not harder. Interfacing with new clients by modem and cell phone has allowed thousands of would-be entrepreneurs to realize their long-time dream of taking control of their futures. Working from home is now a reality for many.

The second edition of this book is all about changes — the increased use of on-line services, virtual marketing on the Internet, new resources, and other new opportunities. More than ever before we have to stay educated on the advancements in technology, the changes in the marketplace, and the opportunities that lie just around the corner. *Develop and Market Your Creative Ideas* will help you meet these needs and allow you to focus on the many opportunities ahead.

Even though I have taken every effort to remain as updated as possible in this second edition, business and government agencies often change addresses and phone numbers. If you encounter difficulty in reaching a number listed in this book's many resource sections, contact directory assistance and request updated information.

DALE DAVIS

June 1996

Acknowledgments

A writer is only a small part of the creative efforts which must mesh together to create a book. Without the special talents of many hard working and sometimes unrecognized individuals, a book would never exist.

It is with my deepest appreciation that I acknowledge and thank these co-workers who have added so much to bring this book together. I would especially like to thank C. C. Dickinson for her fresh new design of the second edition and skillful management of this project.

I would further like to thank Steve Burns for a wonderful cover design; Vickie Reierson, Linda Pinkham, and Sean P. Murray for their editing skills; Jan Olsson for the clean look of each page; Dave Myers for his promotional efforts; and Emmett Ramey for giving me the opportunity to work with such a fine group of talented people.

Preface to the First Edition

I have always had the facility to dream up new ideas. I can't remember a time in my life when I wasn't dreaming about something. In fact, my dreaming has become an important part of my life. When I decided I wanted to be an inventor — a career well-suited for dreamers — I discovered dreams alone would never be enough. To see their visions take flight, dreamers, inventors, and most enterprising people need more. They need to be marketers, researchers, patent agents, financiers, model makers, production specialists, advertisers, brokers, and just plain lucky.

So begins the challenge. If you have an idea and you are determined to get your idea to market, you will have to acquire knowledge of each of these skills and more. If you are enterprising and creative and you have the courage to endure, then your dream, new idea, or concept is only the beginning of an adventure — an adventure filled with battles to fight, mountains to climb, and seemingly impossible obstacles to overcome. You could even imagine your adventure in developing and marketing your idea as being similar to a medieval knight fighting dragons or on a holy quest. The only difference is that self-confidence is your lance, and knowledge and determination are your armor. If you are to be beaten, it is doubt, inexperience, and lack of knowledge that represent today's dragons.

As a self-taught entrepreneur and inventor, I strongly believe in doing as much as possible yourself. If you put yourself to the test of learning new skills, you will greatly improve your chances of success. If you believe you can, half the battle is won. You may be able to hire experience, but you can't hire desire. It is much easier to give instructions than it is to convey your feelings about that idea or dream. I am not saying that you have to become an expert in every field. Sometimes, it is beneficial to hire professionals during certain phases of development. I am, however, suggesting you learn as much as possible to promote your own success, and in the long run, it will be worth a lot more to you than any skilled professional — whom you may not be able to afford anyway.

This book can be both teacher and guide for the adventure ahead. You will examine both the talent and resources needed to bring an idea to life. There is, however, one thing I cannot give you, and that is the motivation and determination you will have to get from within. I strongly believe that the power of a dream is unmatchable and that with a winning idea and determination, you will succeed.

Good teachers can point the way and share their experiences with others. I understand that what works for some people does not necessarily work for others. Whatever I say in this book is based upon my own experience and the experience of hundreds of other inventors, businesspeople, and entrepreneurs I have worked with over the years. These experiences are meant to guide you, but your own insight and ability will often show you new paths that may be even better suited for you.

Part of the great adventure about creating and developing new ideas and dreams is the freedom to experiment and explore. You may decide to play it safe or risk all in your quest for success, but the decision has to be yours. And only you will feel the way an inventor feels when success finally arrives. Many inventors will fail on their first invention, only to learn from their experience and succeed with their next idea. The experience of a failed attempt should never be considered a failure, because the experience you gain will follow you for the rest of your life. Remember, Thomas Edison came up with hundreds of wrong ways to make a light bulb before he finally succeeded. For the dreamer who is not afraid to fail, there is a spirit inside that will not let you stay down, no matter what. Before you know it, another adventure is on its way and you are seeking more dragons to slay.

DALE DAVIS

1991

Introduction

If necessity is the mother of invention, then perseverance is the father. It is a long journey from dream to success, with many ups and downs along the way. So know where you are going and plan ahead. If you just want to "tinker," the experience is the reward, but most would probably like some financial rewards as well. Taking an idea to market must be managed as if it were a business, and as such, your business will have to be marketable if you are going to be successful for any length of time.

Once you have defined your idea, and even your purpose or goal, and believe that the idea does have a market, then it is time to get to work profiting from that idea. Before you start raking in the money, though, you must create a prototype, work out the "bugs," and consider different types of protection for your innovation. You must research, market, finance, and even license it. And that is where it gets interesting.

How to Use this Book

The purpose of this book is to assist and guide the new entrepreneur, inventor, or creative thinker through the different processes that take an idea from conception to market. Before the idea becomes worth anything and the dream becomes reality, there are steps that must be taken along the way. Without these steps, ideas usually go nowhere. Many creative people will need guidance in many marketing and development areas, because often our creative nature does not prepare us for the world of business; that is what this book is all about. It explains the process you will need to go through and, hopefully, provides some inspiration to try out your ideas. You will learn about each facet of bringing an idea to reality, and how to apply each of these aspects to your own idea. Even though the book cannot answer every question, it tries its best to leave no stone unturned. If you supply the necessary determination, the next success story may be yours.

1

Evaluate Your Ideas

The highest reward for a person's toil is not what they get for it, but what they become by it. — John Ruskin

Introduction

Entrepreneurs, inventors, or otherwise creative people often look at life differently than most. They always seem to have a dream and are driven by a desire only they can fully understand. But most of all, they are dreamers.

Dreamers of the past, present, and future all share a special kinship; their dreams are an important part of creativity and innovative ideas — ideas which benefit everyone. Thomas Edison was a dreamer. He dreamed of a longer-lasting lamp that could be operated by electricity. He believed in this innovation, and despite thousands of failures, his dream finally became reality. The lazy and indifferent will never see dreams come true. Only the ambition that comes from personal drive and desire will turn dreams into reality.

Nearly everyone is born with an inquiring and active mind, full of wonder and curiosity. You can see this wonder and curiosity in how children perceive the world around them. Most people caught up in their daily routines take the world's beauty and wonder for granted. Their ability to be inspired and awed by the world around them is surely a gift many lose all too soon by growing older.

But for the inventor or entrepreneur starting a new business or developing an idea, some of that wonder remains. That is why they still dream and believe that they can make a difference. The trouble is, dreams do not pay the bills — ideas are not tangible, and therefore, they are worth little if not developed. In the business world, only profits count. There will be no one applauding your efforts to improve life. The rewards you get will come from seeing your ideas become successes. Then the rewards will come in more ways than you can count.

A decade ago, 73 percent of new industries were created by more than twelve million entrepreneurs with a dream. Since then, entrepreneurs have been forming alliances among themselves and using technology to make their presence known on a global scale. Home workers alone now number more than 43 million, spending more than $60 billion a year on other business services and products.[1] Yet for every success, there are hundreds of failures that you never hear about.

Failure is not a topic many like to discuss. Few authors write business books about failure, and yet, most successes result from earlier failures. Many people may like the inspiration they receive from hearing success stories, but they learn the most from experiencing failure. So don't expect quick success just because you have a dream — it won't happen. Your idea or concept will be tested time and time again; your chances of passing the test will depend on your determination and willingness to learn and adapt. Then you will be headed in the right direction. You would rather say you at least tried than ask, "I wonder if I could have been a success?"

Start a File on Your Idea

If you are really going to take your idea to market or develop your dream further, you must first get in the habit of working with your invention, idea, or new business concept in an organized manner. The first thing to do is start a file. If you do not have a file cabinet or can't get one, use a shoe box or other type of container to hold all your papers and notes regarding your idea. In other words, put everything that has to do with your idea in one place.

If you are one of those inventors who has literally hundreds of ideas and are still coming up with more, start another file for those other current ideas and future projects, and set it aside. Most importantly, pick one idea, and only one. Developing an idea for the market is hard enough without distractions.

---

[1] Helmis, Bruce. *Home Worker Magazine*. Nov./Dec. 1995.

Define Your Idea

One of the first items you will need to file is a written description of your idea. This may not be as simple as it sounds. If a certain process is required to make your invention, research the process; explain the reason for that particular process and why similar processes will not work. Chapter 5, which examines your prototype, will help you with this and even explain the different processes available to you. Write out why you feel your creation is better than existing products, and list its features and advantages.

Defining your idea serves a couple of different purposes. Many inventors and creative thinkers have a tendency to let others worry about the details, even when those details are the obstacles that may keep the idea from the market.

Another purpose for defining your idea lies in the knowledge you will gain by having to understand a process well enough to explain it. For example, people may think a particular item needed for manufacturing as being very inexpensive, not realizing that the tooling cost, set-up charges, and raw stock can cost thousands of dollars up front. The cost of tooling is often added into the manufacturing cost, thus increasing its retail cost.

Understanding these circumstances could help you determine how to develop and market your new idea.

What Is It?

In defining your idea, for example, don't just say that it is a plastic part. Explain what kind of plastic is used and why. Who have you talked with to determine which plastic should be used? Have you compared polyethylene to polypropylene? Do you know the price per pound of each plastic and its properties? To help you with the details, obtain a catalog from a plastics company; most such catalogs will have plastics properties charts in the back. Plastic is only an example here — all materials involved in the development of your idea should be researched in the same manner.

What Does It Do?

In addition to defining what your invention is, you must also define what it does. The same fine detail should be used here as in your definition. When writing out what it does, you should also explain why other means will not work as well. Answer such questions as:

- Why should someone use your product and another?
- What are the advantages of using your product?
- How does your product really stand up to the competition?

Who Will Use It?

In addition to listing all of the above information, you need to also list the potential customer. It is not as simple as merely stating that everyone will use the product. Rather, indicate how people are going to find out about it. Are they going to read about your idea in a magazine, or are they going to see it on television? Do you know what it is going to cost to advertise? Write to various media (newspaper, magazine, radio, and television) to obtain information on advertising rates.

You need to also research and define the demographics of your potential customers. For example, what age, income level, or types of interests will your potential customers have? You need to have a firm understanding of who will be most interested in buying your product and why. To begin your market research, go to your local library and ask the reference desk librarians which publications they have that might be helpful. Chapter 4 discusses how to research your idea.

How Is It Unique?

By the time you have recorded all these details about your idea, you will probably find yourself more knowledgeable about it than before you started the written definition. Do the features still hold up against the competition? The market will be a tough place, and you need to be competitive. Your product has to be unique to really stand out. Considering that most advertising is written, you now understand the importance of a complete and accurate written description of your idea and product.

Make an Objective Evaluation

One of the most difficult tasks creative people can be asked to do is evaluate their own idea. Much like calling your own baby ugly, it just can't be done. If you take your idea to 20 strangers and they all hate it, you have an objective opinion that may help you create an even better new product. Remember, you can always improve on an idea. However, having a good idea does not mean the market is ready for it. Many creative people have come up with ideas ahead of their time. Some take years to develop and market while others literally become an overnight success. There are no perfect ideas; bad ideas have made it to the market and good ideas still remain in someone's closet. The reason for an objective evaluation at this point is so all your energy will be spent focused in the right direction.

When you take your idea to objective people for review — be it through a survey or demonstration — be sure to record all the results and file them in the appropriate place. Chapter 6 is helpful in giving you ways to test market your idea or product.

Helpful Inventor Resources

Additional information about inventions and developing ideas can be obtained by joining or visiting an inventors' organization in your area. To help you find an inventors' organization in your state or to find other information sources for inventors, refer to Appendix A. In addition to Appendix A, you may find valuable assistance and information from government organizations and inventor-oriented publications.

Government Organizations

In addition to inventor organizations, governmental organizations can also help you by giving independent evaluations and assistance.

Business Assistance Service
U.S. Department of Commerce
14th and Constitution, Room 5062
Washington, DC 20230
(202) 482-3176

This service helps guide a small business to the federal agency that can best serve its needs.

FEDIX
(301) 258-0953 (Washington, DC)
(800) 783-3349 (Nationwide)

These phone numbers provide access to procurement and other research information.

National Innovation Workshops – NIWs
Headquartered out of the OERI (see address below), NIWs are inventors' seminars given throughout the country on topics such as patents, licensing, marketing, raising money, and sources of assistance. To find out more on NIWs, contact the OERI or your local Small Business Development Center (SBDC).

National Technology Transfer Center
316 Washington Avenue
Wheeling, WV 26003
(304) 243-2455
(304) 243-2560 (*Business Gold On-line*)
(800) 678-6882 (Nationwide)

This center is a clearinghouse for government technical information. It will assist businesses in development of new products and provide connections with licensable technology. It also provides *Business Gold On-line Service* — access to information on federal technology and research opportunities.

Office of Energy-Related Inventions – OERI
National Bureau of Standards – Institute of Applied Technology
U.S. Department of Commerce
Washington, DC 20234
(202) 586-5000
FAX (202) 586-5049

The OERI provides services for energy-related inventions and possible funding.

Service Corps of Retired Executives – SCORE
U.S. Small Business Administration
1441 L Street NW, Room 100
Washington, DC 20416
(800) 827-5722 (Nationwide)

SCORE is comprised of retired executives who offer sound advice based on their years of experience. Contact this SCORE office for the office nearest you.

Technology Utilization Programs
National Aeronautics & Space Administration – NASA
4200 Forbes Boulevard., Suite 106
Lanham, MD 20706-4342
(301) 918-8150
FAX (301) 918-8154

This agency provides small business innovation research funding.

Publications

You may also find newsletters and other publications that deal with innovation are very helpful resources when trying to research product development. Here is a brief listing of some publications available to you.

The Business Owner
383 South Broadway
Hicksville, NY 11801
(800) 634-0605 (Nationwide)

Business Start-Ups/Entrepreneur Magazine
Subscriber Service
P.O. Box 58932
Boulder, CO 80322
(800) 421-2300 (Nationwide)

Dream Merchant Magazine
2309 Torrance Boulevard, Suite 201
Torrance, CA 90501
(800) 35 DREAM
FAX (310) 328-1844

The Guerrilla Marketing Newsletter
P.O. Box 1336
Mill Valley, CA 94942
(800) 748-6444 (Nationwide)

IDEAS Digest News Magazine
1220-808 Nelson Street
Box 12151
Vancouver, BC V6Z 2H2
(604) 689-3626
FAX (604) 684-4589

"INVENT" Journal of the Inventors' Workshop International
Mind Sight Data
8 West Janss Road
Thousand Oaks, CA 91360
(805) 497-4053

Invention Connection/Inventor's Voice
Invention Services International Corp./Journal and News Service
P.O. Box 93669
Los Angeles, CA 90093-0669
(213) 878-6925
(800) 458-5624 (Nationwide)
FAX (213) 962-8588

Inventors' Digest
2132 East Bijou Street
Colorado Springs, CO 80909
(719) 635-1234

Nation's Business
U.S. Department of Commerce
1615 H Street, NW
Washington, DC 20062
(202) 463-5650
(800) 638-6582 (Nationwide)

Sensors
174 Concord Street
Peterborough, NH 03458
(603) 924-9631
FAX (603) 924-7408

Small Business Reports
American Management Association
P.O. Box 51136
Boulder, CO 80322-3140
(800) 234-1094 (Nationwide)

Tech Access Report
5723 Nebraska Avenue, NW
Washington, DC 20015
(202) 244-4191

Technical Aid for Small Business Manufacturers
409 Third Street, SW, Room 7600
Washington, DC 20416
(202) 205-6740

Technology Access Report
16 Digital Drive, Suite 250
Novato, CA 94949
(800) 733-1556 (Nationwide)
FAX (415) 883-6421

2

Patents

Success is more attitude than aptitude. — Unknown

Intellectual Property

Somewhere between your conception of a new idea and marketing your invention, you must investigate what form of protection you will need to obtain regarding your product. This decision will require an understanding of the many types of intellectual property. Intellectual property is also referred to as intangible property, proprietary assets, industrial property, or proprietary rights.

Intellectual property includes items such as patents, trademarks, copyrights, trade secrets, and trade names. Intellectual property laws govern these areas of business, and when necessary, are used in court to determine intellectual property rights. Intellectual property laws cover all forms of protection, ranging from patent infringements to unfair competition.

Defending Intellectual Property

If you have intellectual property, it may mean you will someday have to defend your rights to the property in a court of law. Before the mid-1970s, patents were deemed invalid in approximately 73 percent of the cases taken to court. As a result, inventors — previously having only a 27 percent chance in court — lost respect for patents. The lack of enforceability of U.S. patents resulted in a 34 percent decline in the number of patents awarded to Americans between 1972 and 1982.

Today, the trend seems to be moving in favor of the inventor. Currently, there are no criminal penalties for patent infringement; however, the following civil remedies do exist:

- An injunction against future infringement; and
- Compensatory damages — in no event, less than a reasonable royalty.

In response to the growing number of court battles fought over intellectual property rights, some insurance companies now offer patent infringement insurance. Unfortunately, this type of insurance is quite expensive — annual premiums range between $150,000 and $200,000 for $5 million of liability and legal expense coverage.

According to the Administration Office of the U.S. Courts, patent infringement cases filed in federal court in 1992 alone represent a 75 percent increase over the number of cases filed a decade earlier.

Some of the decisions handed down by courts in recent years, however, have discouraged infringers from litigating an infringement suit. Some of these decisions include:

- In *Lemelson vs. Mattel*, a jury found that Mattel had infringed on a Lemelson patent and awarded $70 million in damages.
- General Motors had to pay $8.8 million in damages — and more than $11 million in pre- and post-judgment interest — for infringement on a lubricating process patent.
- Smith International was ordered to pay $205 million for infringing a Hughes Tool patent.

Before considering whether an infringement suit is warranted, consider that many cases will require years to complete and may proceed from the U.S. District Court to a U.S. Court of Appeals for the Federal Circuit, and may even be taken to the U.S. Supreme Court. The cost involved in these court proceedings can be staggering.

Although patents are often the subject of infringement suits, copyrights, trademarks, trade secrets, and unfair competition may also be subjected to the same proceedings.

Protect Your Idea — Keep a Logbook

Creating a paper trail is one of the oldest and most inexpensive ways of protecting your invention. Most importantly, you want to document your invention's date of conception. One of the best ways of doing this is to obtain and use an inventor's logbook. The ideal logbook is bound or stitched so its pages cannot be removed. In this case, the pages would have to be used consecutively. A looseleaf notebook, for instance, would not work. One easy way to start an inventor's logbook is to purchase a daily planner at any stationery or business supply store and use it as a log.

Your logbook, properly maintained, can be used as documentation in the event of a legal dispute, and therefore, should not be taken lightly. Start writing in your inventor's logbook as soon as possible after you conceive the idea. Further, the inventor's logbook is more than a means of effectively documenting the date of conception — it also serves you well in recording test results, successful prototypes, and failures. A well-kept logbook will include your thoughts, sketches, notes, calculations, telephone numbers, and contacts.

For the logbook to stand up in court, it is advisable to document everything so that anyone reading it can easily understand and comprehend the information. Remember, once an invention is described in detail, you should date and sign the appropriate page or pages, and have your signature notarized or witnessed. If it seems risky to have your logbook notarized, remember that the notary is merely witnessing your signature and the date, and does not need to see or understand the information contained in your logbook regarding your invention. Although keeping a logbook and having it notarized occasionally may seem somewhat troublesome, the logbook's ultimate importance will be determined by your invention's possibilities and your diligence in maintaining it properly.

Even if you never have to use your logbook for legal matters, its importance cannot be understated or diminished. Sometimes, going back six months in the logbook to locate an old telephone number or contact can have real value in itself.

Guidelines for Maintaining a Logbook

These guidelines will help you maintain a quality logbook.

- Keep a separate logbook for each project you work on, and make notes each time you work on your invention.
- Once your idea is developed to some potential, describe it and have the description notarized or witnessed.

- Keep all records — such as telephone numbers, contacts, addresses, notes, tests, and any reference material — in your logbook.
- Do not leave blank pages. Present the information in your logbook chronologically to maintain its validity.
- When demonstrating a prototype to a witness, have the witness give a written description of the operation and the results observed. The witness should then sign and date the appropriate page or pages.

Keeping a logbook is a common practice of engineers, designers, and research and development personnel who want to maintain clear and accurate records of the genesis and progress of their ideas.

Disclosure Document Program

The disclosure document program is for the inventor who wishes to obtain alternative or additional protection of an idea. The program is administered by the U.S. Patent and Trademark Office, which accepts and preserves your invention disclosure document in strict confidence for a period of two years, or longer, if your patent application refers to the disclosure. The purpose of this service is to provide a credible form of evidence, should you need it. Originally, this service was intended to stop inventors from mailing a description of their own inventions to themselves, which they believed to be a valid form of protection — it is not.

The disclosure document is not a substitute for a patent application and should not be considered a grace period for filing the application. The program is aimed at allowing inventors to feel protected enough to proceed with their ideas, rather than hiding or sitting on them. Just like an inventor's logbook, a disclosure document can be upheld in court and can ultimately resolve a patent infringement case.

Filing a Disclosure Document

To file a disclosure document, you first need to send a description of your invention on an 8 1/2 X 11-inch sheet of paper (or a copy from your logbook). The description is important. It must be limited to written matter or drawings on paper or other thin, flexible material, such as linen, plastic, or mylar, having dimensions — or folded to dimensions — not to exceed 8 1/2 X 13 inches.

Next, number each page. Text and drawings should be sufficiently dark and bold to permit reproduction with commonly used office copying machines. Photographs may be submitted, but they are not required. You may also want to have the disclosure document notarized. Send your description — along with a check or money order for $10 payable to the Commissioner of Patents and Trademarks. Include a stamped, self-addressed envelope and the below signed request in duplicate.

> *"The undersigned, being the inventor of the disclosed invention, requests that the enclosed papers be accepted under the disclosure document program and that they be preserved for a period of two years."*

Commissioner of Patents and Trademarks
Washington, DC 20231

When received by the U.S. Patent and Trademark Office, your disclosure document will be stamped with an identification number and the date of receipt. The duplicate request will then be returned to you in the self-addressed envelope, together with a notice indicating that the disclosure document may be relied upon only as evidence, and that a patent application should be filed if patent protection is desired. The disclosure document program does not diminish the value of your notarized and witnessed records as evidence of the conception date of your invention; it does, however, provide the U.S. Patent and Trademark Office with a credible form of evidence that can be referred to in a separate letter in the patent application, should you decide to file within the two-year period.

Patents

A patent is a grant that results from a contract with the U.S. government, whereby the inventor agrees to disclose his or her invention to the public to further technology. In return, the government grants the inventor the right to exclude all others from making and selling the product for a certain period of time. A patent generally allows an inventor the right to exclude others from making and selling the product for 17 years, provided that maintenance fees are paid every 3 1/2 years.

If maintenance fees are not paid after the first 3 1/2 years, as well as at 7 1/2 and 12 years, the patent becomes void and public domain. While patents are considered a grant or contract with the government, they actually offer no rights at all. Patents do offer the right to keep others from using or selling the patented invention, but they do not offer the monopoly many believe to coexist with patents. Patents are in a sense a license to litigate, or, in other words, a reason to sue.

Why, then, would anyone want to obtain a patent? To sue others? To keep infringers at bay? A patent will become a most expensive asset even if you win your lawsuits. If, instead, your reasons for patenting an invention or idea are to obtain protection and a marketing tool, you will find that a patent can become a tremendous asset.

History of Patents

Patent law in the United States has an interesting history, which began in 1790 when the first patent laws were adopted. Our forefathers recognized the need to protect new ideas, and created a specific provision authorizing a grant of protection for a limited time to authors and inventors. This provision, Article 2, Section 8, became effective March 4, 1789, and was implemented April 10, 1790, by George Washington, thus giving Congress the power to promote the useful arts.

Since then, the laws have changed a number of times. One important change came in 1952, allowing a patent to be issued for a new use of an old device. But the basic concept of providing an exclusive right to an inventor has always remained the same.

The United States was not the first nation to adopt such laws on patents. In fact, the historical development of patents can be traced back to ancient Greek and Roman times. The first patent in recorded history was granted in the ancient Greek colony of Sybusis in 500 B.C. for a gourmet dish. During the Dark Ages, patents seemed to disappear and very little innovation, if any, took place. However, during the latter part of the Middle Ages, procedures were again organized to protect inventors and improve technology.

In the 1300s, new ideas used in the design and construction of canals, bridges, and mills in Venice were protected. In 1330, France offered a royal degree to inventors for developing ideas and inventions. By the year 1500, inventions and patents flourished in the Italian states and the German Empire.

Thereafter, the custom of granting patents was adopted in the Netherlands and England. From England, patents were extended into the American Colonies. Until 1790, patents were granted by a colony to its citizens. In receiving a patent, inventors obtained a grant from the U.S. government for a limited monopoly. The first U.S. patent was issued on July 31, 1790, to Samuel Hopkins for a process for making "pot and pearl ashes."

The U.S. Patent and Trademark Office, established in 1802, was initially operated under the Department of State. In 1849, the office was placed under the authority of the Department of the Interior, and in 1925, under the Department of Commerce. For the first 80 years of its existence, the U.S. Patent and Trademark Office required a working model of an invention in order to issue a patent.

New Patent Laws

Patent laws have gone through considerable changes recently due to the United States implementing the Uruguay Round Agreement of the General Agreement on Tariffs and Trade (GATT), which was negotiated by the U.S. trade representative and representatives from 110 other countries. Congress passed the new laws in November 1994, and President Clinton signed them on December 8, 1994. The changes align the U.S. patent system with the systems in most other industrialized countries and clear the way for the United States to join the World Trade Organizations.

According to the U.S. Patent and Trademark Office, for all patents issued from applications filed on or after June 8, 1995, the patent rights will begin when the patent is granted and end 20 years from the day the inventor filed the patent application. If the applications are contentious, continuations-in-part, or divisional, the term will end 20 years after the date of the earliest filed patent, nonprovisional application.

Regarding patents issued from applications filed before June 8, 1995, the patent term will expire in either 20 years from the earliest U.S. filing date or 17 years from the date the patent is granted, whichever is longer. On patents that are in force on June 8, 1995, the new patent laws specify that the term will be the greater of either 20 years from the earliest U.S. filing date or 17 years from the date of the patent grant.

A New Provisional Patent

One major change provided in the new patent laws includes a provisional patent application. As of June 8, 1995, inventors will be able to file a provisional application, which will allow them to obtain an early filing date with few formalities and at a lower cost than filing a nonprovisional application. This new application differs from a nonprovisional application because the patent term does not start from this filing date; the application is not examined; and it cannot issue as a patent.

The provisional application is retained in confidence and is automatically abandoned twelve months after filing. Before the provisional application expires, the applicant must file a nonprovisional application to obtain a patent.

Inventors filing a provisional application must still clearly define their invention in writing and include drawings, but the filing fee for a small entity is only $75. The inventor then has up to twelve months to file a nonprovisional patent application and claim the benefits of the provisional application filing date.

If you would like specific details about provisional patent applications, contact:

U.S. Patent and Trademark Office
(703) 305-9300

Today, three types of nonprovisional patents are available: utility patents, design patents, and living plant patents.

Utility Patents

If your invention relates to a functional aspect of any machine, process, method, article, or composition, the best method of protection may be the utility patent.

Utility patents are by far the most common of all patents and protect everything from new machinery to genetically altered animals. There are some 400 different categories for utility patents, covering such items as hardware, toys, tools, vehicles, sporting goods, time- and labor-saving devices, and cooking implements.

With the exception of items covered by the Atomic Energy Act of 1954, which excludes the patenting of inventions used solely in the manufacture of nuclear or atomic weapons, nearly everything can be classed into the patent classification system. The patent classification system is discussed in further detail later in this chapter.

Design Patents

If you believe that your invention has a unique ornamental appearance and you would like to protect its external appearance, then a design patent is the way to go. Design patents are not only easier to apply for and receive, but are far less costly than a utility patent.

To be patentable as a design patent, your invention's appearance must not be obvious — that is, someone with ordinary skills in your field would not easily design the same appearance. Because many past inventors have used design patents when their inventions did not qualify for a utility patent, design patents have an image of being somewhat weak in nature or second rate, but this is not true.

Design patents allow the same rights as a utility patent and allow you to use the patent-pending status and to license your invention, as does a utility patent.

A design patent is only applicable to aesthetics or ornamental features; the design in itself may have no significant functional purpose. The design must be inseparable from the invention and cannot be a surface ornamentation, such as a cover or label.

A good example of a design that could be patented is a tire tread design. The tread offers a design feature to the tire, which by itself would be unpatentable. The design patent on the tread would protect your invention from infringers using any similar designs. Design patent applications consist of a drawing, appropriate forms, and a $155 filing fee if you are an individual inventor or small company.

Plant Patents

The Plant Patents Act of 1930 amended U.S. patent law to permit protection of any new and distinct variety of asexually reproduced plants, other than tuber-propagated plants. This legislation supported the plant breeders who are few in number, yet important to the advancement of agriculture.

Plant patents cover all new varieties of plants produced asexually from cutting and grafting and, unlike with utility patents, usefulness is not a requirement for patentability. One of the better known plant patents is for the Santa Rosa plum, developed by Luther Burbank, who also created the Burbank potato, which, incidentally, was introduced into Ireland to help combat the blight epidemic. Burbank originated more than 800 new strains of peaches, prunes, berries, and lilies. Plant patents, though rare, are still very important to today's agricultural market.

Qualifying for a Patent

In discussing the patentability of your invention, consider this passage from United States Code Title 35-101 under Inventions Patentable:

> *"Whoever invents or discovers any new and useful process, machine, manufacture, or composition of matter, or any new and useful improvement thereof, may obtain a patent thereof, subject to the conditions and requirements of this title."*

Title 35-102 further dictates conditions for patentability, including:

- The invention cannot be known or used by others, or patented or described in a printed publication anywhere before the inventor applies for a patent.
- The invention cannot be used in public or be on sale for more than one year before application for a patent.
- The invention cannot be abandoned in another application.
- The invention cannot already be patented for more than one year in a foreign country.
- The invention cannot be described in another patent or application.
- The invention cannot be invented by someone else.

In determining the priority of inventions that have been filed at the same time, not only will the respective dates of conception and the reduction to practice be considered, but also the reasonable diligence of who was first to put the invention into practice.

Should there be an interference in patents, the U.S. Patent and Trademark Office will evaluate who actually did the most to commercialize the invention. The United States is the only country that awards patents to the first to conceive, not the first to patent.

After examining some of the requirements necessary for you to obtain a patent, it may be easier to understand what is not patentable. For example, you cannot patent:

- An idea, as opposed to a mechanical device;
- A method of doing business;

- Printed matter that you would copyright;
- Inoperable devices, such as perpetual motion machines, without working prototypes;
- An obvious improvement, such as using plastic to replace steel;
- Illegal inventions, such as a money-making machine or a new safe-cracking explosive;
- Nuclear weapons [hopefully, no one would worry about this];
- Theoretical matter, such as the Big Bang Theory;
- Subject matter that falls under trademarks or copyrights; or
- Untested drugs, which require Food and Drug Administration (FDA) approval to be patentable.

With these guidelines, it should now be much easier to determine if your idea is patentable.

How to Apply for a Patent

To obtain a patent, you must file an application with the federal government asking that it find the subject matter described in the application new, useful, and unobvious. Contact a patent agent to assist you in the preparation of a patent application, or, file one yourself, using one of the self-help books available.

In particular, you can obtain *Patent It Yourself* by David Pressman. You can order the book from your local bookstore or contact its publisher directly.

Nolo Press
950 Parker Street
Berkeley, CA 94710-9867
(510) 549-1976
(800) 992-6656 (Nationwide)

A word of warning when filing for your own patent: Become knowledgeable about the process before you start, or you may place your patent at risk. This is not to say that you should not file for your own patent. On the contrary, many believe the inventor is the best person to do so, providing he or she is serious enough to become knowledgeable in the matter.

Writing a patent application can be an art form all its own, and it should be well researched to be effective.

Patent Application Contents

A patent application consists of these six main items.

1. Specifications, including:
   a. The title of your invention;
   b. Background or history of the invention;
   c. The invention's features, advantages, and objectives;
   d. A brief description of the drawings;
   e. A narrative description of the structure;
   f. An explanation of how the invention works; and
   g. A summary of claims.
2. Drawings.
3. A filing fee, either check or money order.
4. A transmittal (cover) letter.
5. A stamped, self-addressed receipt post card.
6. Forms, including:
   a. A completed *Patent Application Declaration* form;
   b. A *Small Entity Declaration*, if an individual or company has fewer than 500 employees;
   c. An *Information Disclosure Statement*; and
   d. Copies of patents you cited in your application and listed on the *Information Disclosure Statement*.

The forms required for filing a patent application can be obtained from the U.S. Patent and Trademark Office or from your library's book of forms.

Time Requirements for Filing

In the United States, there are several legal requirements before you can obtain a patent. One is that the application must be filed within one year after the invention is first placed in public use, disclosed in a printed publication, or placed on sale. If you do not file within a year, you will have lost your right to file.

For the latest information regarding patents, you can call or write:

Assistant Commissioner for Patents
Crystal Park 2, Suite 910
Washington, DC 20231
(703) 305-8800
FAX (703) 305-8825

Additionally, you can connect via their Internet address.

http://www.uspto.gov/

Ownership of Patents

A patent application must originally be filed in the name of the actual inventor. However, patent rights may be assigned, licensed, or even given away. Assignments must be in writing and must be recorded in the U.S. Patent and Trademark Office within three months of the assignment. In an employment situation, if the employee is hired to invent specific subject matter, any patent obtained on such subject matter would be owned by the employer. Many employees sign contracts that specifically provide for ownership of all patent rights.

Foreign Patents

One hundred seventy-nine nations provide some form of patent protection for new inventions. Patent protection provided by many countries extends to their colonies, territories, and protectorates. An example of this is a U.S. patent, which is enforceable in Eastern Samoa, Guam, the Panama Canal Zone, Puerto Rico, and the Virgin Islands. If your product is headed to another country, a foreign patent may be a necessity.

Fortunately, a U.S. patent application preserves the right to file in a foreign country for a period of one year from the U.S. filing date. An application filed in the United States would give you a priority date if you were to obtain a foreign patent.

The United States and most nations are parties to patent protection treaties which provide reciprocal patent rights to their citizens. One important reciprocal right is the right of priority, whereby foreign patent applications are treated as having been filed on the dates of corresponding

U.S. patent applications on which they are based. Thus, the U.S. filing date can be the effective filing date of most foreign patent applications filed within one year.

In the United States, the patent rights generally belong to the first inventor, but in most foreign countries, they belong to the inventor with the earliest effective patent application. Filing a U.S. patent application usually results in another benefit, such as a foreign filing license.

Shortly after you file your U.S. application, you will probably receive your foreign filing license, which authorizes the filing of a foreign patent application. You can file a foreign patent before filing a U.S. patent. If you do, the one-year filing period runs from the date of the foreign application filing.

If you are interested in filing a foreign patent, you can save thousands of dollars by dealing directly with foreign patent agents. A problem you will encounter when dealing directly with another country will be finding a patent attorney there. Your local library can help you here. Another option would be to send your request by fax, thus avoiding excessive long-distance phone bills.

One patent agent service you may find helpful in applying for a foreign patent is:

Kings Patent Agency
73 Farrington Road
London, England EC1M3JB
(171) 248-6161
FAX (171) 831-0926

When filing foreign patents, consider regional patents as well. Regional patents can be filed with either the European Patent Office (EPO) or the African Intellectual Property Organization (AIPO). EPO patent applications cover Austria, Belgium, France, Germany, Greece, Italy, Liechtenstein, Luxembourg, Netherlands (Holland), Spain, Sweden, Switzerland, and the United Kingdom (England, Wales, Scotland, and Ireland). Although an application is examined by the EPO, each country within the organization issues its own patent.

AIPO patents protect your invention in Benin, Cameroon, Central African Republic, Chad, Congo, Gabon, Mali, Mauritania, Senegal, and Togo. Filing a single EPO or AIPO patent application can be much less expensive than filing individually in each country.

The formation of the EPO and AIPO can be attributed largely to the Patent Cooperation Treaty (PCT). In 1987, the United States adopted important provisions of the PCT, which gave U.S. patent filers these advantages in filing foreign patents.

- The final designation of the foreign countries in which patent coverage is desired can be delayed for up to 30 months after the U.S. filing date.
- With the addition of Canada in 1989, most of the important industrialized nations are now members of the PCT.
- Filing and prosecution of the early phases of a PCT application are entirely in English.
- A PCT patent application can be used to delay the issuance of a U.S. patent or to cause a U.S. application to be published early in the procedure.

On January 1, 1994, the North American Free Trade Agreement (NAFTA) forever changed the relationship between Canada, Mexico, and the United States. NAFTA has made many changes in our international trade laws, including improvements in the protection of intellectual property. NAFTA is designed to help Canada, Mexico, and the United States compete in the emerging global marketplace. By providing international cooperation, the agreement will help in halting pirating and counterfeiting by bringing our separate laws in line with each other.

The United States is not only competing with its neighbors for technology trade, but the world as well. In 1995, Japan received 22,871 patents in the United States, while the total U.S. patents given to Americans numbered 64,509. That is 35 percent of U.S. patents going to Japan alone. In 1995, the rest of the world's countries received 11,395 U.S. patents.[1]

Patent Searches

It is always advisable to conduct a patent search before either retaining legal counsel or filing a patent application yourself. The patent search is your insurance against spending time and money unnecessarily. When

---

[1] Figures based upon March 1996 report from the *U.S. Patent Office Technology Assessment Report*.

doing your patent search, you will either become more aware of just how brilliant your idea really is, or you may find a dozen or more different versions of your idea already patented. Of course, finding similar prior art is not necessarily bad news. The education you get from reviewing other inventions should only assist you in further developing your own invention.

Use a Patent Depository Library

Doing your own patent search is recommended. There are patent depository libraries in each state for doing your search, and the day spent searching and traveling could save you up to $500. For your convenience, a listing of state patent depository libraries is featured in Appendix B, located at the back of this book.

If you really want to dive in head first, go to Arlington, Virginia, and do your search at the U.S. Patent and Trademark Office Science Library. This library contains approximately 28 million documents in the search file, with some 5 million of these being U.S. patents. Dating back to 1790 when the patent system began, this library boasts more than 9 million cross-references and more than 13 million foreign patent documents. In addition, there are more than 120,000 volumes of information in the scientific library, consisting of trade literature, texts, digests, and journals. See Appendix B for the address and other contact information.

There are more than 400 classes of inventions and 120,000 subclasses. Before actually doing your own patent search, you must weigh the considerations, and if you decide to go ahead, have your class and subclass in hand. This is discussed later in this chapter's section on the patent classification system. Be prepared to spend an entire day; it will be both interesting and educational.

If you are not able to get to your city library and use the *Patent Office Manual of Classification*, or are not able to send in your request to the U.S. Patent and Trademark Office, you can look up your class and subclass at the state or patent library, but these manuals are usually in short supply at patent libraries.

Once you have determined your class and subclass, find a patent librarian and request the computer listing of all the patents in your class. The computer listing, which may contain from 30 to 200 patents or more, generally comes from the main patent library in Arlington and will list the patents in which you need to search. The patents are listed chronologically, beginning with the newest patents.

The first thing you may question on your listing is the letters beside certain numbers: "D" indicates that the patent is a design patent; "X" indicates a cross reference; and "RE" indicates a reissue.

Examine the Official Gazette

With this information in hand, you can start your search by examining the abstracts in the *Official Gazette*. The *Official Gazette* is published weekly and lists the patents issued for that week, grouped by general, mechanical, chemical, electrical, design, and reissued patents. This publication offers a means for viewing a summary of the invention, known as an abstract. Along with the abstract, there will also be a drawing, where possible. This abstract allows a more efficient search without your having to dig through the mountains of paperwork on the five million-plus U.S. patents.

The best way to do your search is to look up each listed patent number from top to bottom in the *Official Gazette* and mark the patents of interest. After eliminating the patents that you feel are not relevant, make a list of those patents that you would like to more closely examine.

In many libraries, you may give the librarian the list of relevant patents, and she will make copies of them, usually at a nominal charge. Many librarians may simply direct you to the patent files and copying machine to make your own copies. So be sure to take a pocket full of change. If cost is not an issue and you have the time, the list may also be sent to the U.S. Patent and Trademark Office for copies at the prevailing rates.

One word of warning when doing your search: The day may become quite long and you may find yourself scanning or even missing relevant patents. This may come back to haunt you later. So if you need a break, take one. Remember, it is easier to do it right the first time than make an additional trip later.

Understand the Patent Classification System

The U.S. Patent and Trademark Office maintains a highly sophisticated classification system, arranging patents into more than 400 classes and 120,000 subclasses in chronological order dating back to 1790.

Without this system of classes and subclasses, it would be impossible to make any kind of patent search. A typical class, such as fasteners, can have subclasses, further breaking fasteners down into nail, stapling, or clenching fasteners, to further define and assist in doing a patent search.

Although searching 400 classes and 120,000 subclasses may seem somewhat mind-boggling, the research to find your class and subclass starts with a trip to the public library, to look through the *Patent Office Manual of Classification*. You can also purchase the manual in loose-leaf form, by writing to:

Superintendent of Documents
U.S. Government Printing Office
Washington, DC 20402

Because the patent classification system is so sophisticated, the U.S. Patent and Trademark Office offers a free service to inventors to help find their class and subclass, but this service can take three to eight weeks before you receive a response.

If you do choose to have the U.S. Patent and Trademark Office classify your invention for you, show your name and address at the top of a 8 1/2 X 11-inch sheet of paper. Below that, write: "Please advise me what subject area and/or class(es) and/or subclass(es) cover my intended invention." Then list your invention's features, operation, and intended use. Give accurate details so that your idea is fully understood; otherwise, you may be given an incorrect class or subclass. Once completed, mail the information to:

Commissioner of Patents and Trademarks
Washington, DC 20231

Computer Searches Are Available

Another method of searching patents is through a computer database. Computer patent searches consist of keywords being searched through different databases to match topic matter.

Computer searches can be very effective for doing preliminary searches before going into a more thorough patent search. If you have a personal computer with a modem, or know someone with one, you can perform your own search. Be aware that these databases charge anywhere from $50 to $100 per hour. The first search has a learning curve that will cost you extra money and time. Some services even assess additional service charges of $50 or more for first-time use.

Unless you wish to do several searches, your savings in time may not be worth the trouble and expense of doing the search. Computer searches will give you an abstract, but not a drawing; so consider the type of search you are doing before deciding if computer searching is for you.

If you decide that you would like to give computer searching a try, consult your local library for the latest available service and phone numbers. Many libraries can even perform computer searches for you at very reasonable rates. In addition, some good databases to possibly contact include:

BRS Information Technologies
555 East Lancaster Avenue
St. Davis, PA 19087
(215) 254-0233
(800) 468-0908 (outside of state)

Mead Data Center
9443 Springboro Pike
P.O Box 93
Dayton, OH 45401
(513) 865-6800
(800) 227-1908 (outside of state)

Permagon Infoline, Inc.
1340 Old Chain Bridge Road
McLean, VA 22101
(703) 442-0900
(800) 336-7575 (outside of state)

Refer to Chapter 4 for other commercial on-line databases.

Evaluate Your Search

The patent search can be a very humbling experience. It could be quite a surprise to discover that your "new" idea was in fact patented in 1892. Don't let similar patents discourage you. It would be nearly impossible to go through millions of patents and not find some similar prior art. Any patents that are similar can later be turned into tools. For example, consider the inventor who found out that his invention was 200 years old, yet still not on the market. Intrigued, he made further improvements to his invention using the 200-year-old patent, then decided to put his enhanced idea on the market. Within a year, he had licensed his patent in three countries, using that 200-year-old idea.

Look at the whole picture and use your search as a tool — not a crutch.

Patent Pending

You may ask yourself: "What's going on during the time between applying for a patent, and possibly receiving a patent?"

The fact is, this time period of the patent adventure requires special considerations. If you are proceeding with the marketing of your invention, as you should be, the only legal protection you can obtain is the patent pending label. The patent pending label legally warns would-be patent infringers that a patent has been applied for and may be granted. If, however, you are tempted to use the patent pending label without first filing an application, you can be fined $500 for this federal offense.

If you have a patent, you have the right to take an infringer to court. If you have a patent pending, you only have the right to tell would-be infringers that when a patent is granted, you intend to take them to court. In order to get an infringer to court, you will have to bear the cost of an attorney and all court costs until you can prove guilt.

Any judgment to stop an infringer will provide damages equal to 50 percent of his or her earnings from your invention. The infringer's loss is usually only in the tooling used to produce your invention. Generally, infringers settle out of court by buying a license to continue producing your invention.

One thing to consider before taking an infringer to court is that a percentage of infringers will take the offensive and try to invalidate your patent. Your patent's validity can be questioned in court by finding prior art similar to yours which was not discussed in your application. And with five million patents to search through, the chances are there that something similar will be found.

The truth of the matter is, patent pending does not strike fear into the heart of the would-be infringer. Patent pending is really aimed at keeping the honest company honest. The point here is to put your faith in the invention and not the possible patent. If your plan is to license your invention, remember that an existing market has more bargaining power than a proposed patent.

While your invention is pending patent, explore the market, even if only in a limited fashion, and work on establishing a trademark, trade dress, marketing studies, and even licensing. Inventions can be licensed before the patent application has been filed.

You need to consider the importance and potential of your invention far more than the potential of a patent. You will find when approaching the marketplace that your invention will evolve according to market influences. In some cases, the market influences the invention so much that the original patent is abandoned, and a new invention is created and patented.

Depending on the invention, new improvements needed for marketing your invention can even be incorporated into an existing patent application. During office actions, claims will be amended and strengthened, sometimes even allowing new subject matter, if done properly.

Patent Publications

To help you with the patent process, the U.S. Patent and Trademark Office in Washington, D.C., has a number of useful publications you can request.

- *The Disclosure Document Program*
- *General Information Concerning Patents*
- *General Information Concerning Trademarks*
- *Guide for Patent Draftsmen*
- *Patent Profiles*

Acronyms

Some of the acronyms listed on the following pages may be unfamiliar to you so to help you understand their meaning, first is a brief glossary of these terms. As you go through the process of bringing your new idea to the marketplace, these acronyms will become more familiar.

- APS, Automated Patent System.
- EPO, European Patent Office.
- IPEA, International Preliminary Examining Authority.

- ISA, International Search Authority.
- JPO, Japan Patent Office.
- PCT, Patent Cooperation Treaty.
- PTO, Patent and Trademark Office.
- SIR, Statutory Invention Registration.
- WIPO, World Intellectual Property Organization.

Patent Filing and Processing Costs

Shown on the following pages are the fees charged, as of October 1, 1995, by the U.S. Patent and Trademark Office for filing a patent application. The fees shown are for small businesses — those with fewer than 500 employees.

Filing Fees	
Utility patent	$ 375
Design patent	155
Plant patent	255
Claims	
Independent claims in excess of three	$ 39 each
Claims in excess of 20	11 each
Multiple dependent claims	125
Reissue Application Fee	$ 375
Response Extension Fees	
One month	$ 55
Two months	190
Three months	450
Four months	700
Appeals and Hearings Fees	
Notice of appeal	$ 145
Brief in support of appeal	145
Oral hearing request	125

Issue Fees	
Utility patent	$ 625
Design patent	215
Plant patent	315

Maintenance Fees (utility patents only)	
At 3 1/2 years	$ 495
At 7 1/2 years	995
At 12 years	1,495

Other patent fees that may also be incurred include the following:

Patent Fees	
Surcharge for late oath or declaration	$ 65
Reissue independent claims over original patent	39 each
Reissue claims in excess of 20 and over	11 each
Non-English specification	130

Maintenance Fees	
Surcharge – late payment within six months	$ 65
Unavoidable late payment on expired patent	660
Unintentional late payment on expired patent	1,550

Miscellaneous Fees	
Extension of term of patent	$1,060
Certificate of correction	100
Request for reexamination	2,390
Statutory disclaimer	55

Patent Petition Fees	
Petition to the Commissioner	$ 130
Submission of *Information Disclosure Statement*	220
Petition for public use proceeding	1,430
Petition to revive unavoidably abandoned application	55
Petition to revive unintentionally abandoned application	625

PCT Fees

Late filing fee or oath or declaration	$ 65
English translation after 20 months	130
IPEA – U.S.	340
ISA – U.S.	375
PTO – not ISA or IPEA	505
Claims meet PCT	47
Claims – extra independent (over three)	39 each
Claims – extra total (over twenty)	11 each
Claims – multiple dependent	125
For filing with EPO or JPO search report	440

PCT Fees – International Stage

Transmittal fee	$ 220
PCT search fee – no U.S. application	660
Supplemental search per additional invention	190
PCT search – prior U.S. application	430
Preliminary examination fee – ISA was the U.S.	470
Preliminary examination fee – ISA not the U.S.	710
Additional invention – ISA was the U.S.	140
Additional invention – ISA not the U.S.	250

PCT Fees to WIPO

Basic fee (first 30 pages)	$ 604
Basic supplemental fee (for each page over 30)	12
Handling fee	185
Designation fee per country	147

PCT Fees to EPO

International search	$1,722

Patent Service Fees

Printed copy of patent w/o color, regular service	$ 3
Printed copy of patent w/o color, expedited local service	6
Printer copy of patent w/o color, EPO expedited	25
Printed copy of plant patent, in color	12

Patent Service Fees (continued)	
Copy of utility patent or SIR, w/color drawings	24
Copy of application as filed, regular service	15
Copy of application as filed, expedited local service	30
Copy of patent-related file wrapper and contents	150
Copy of document, unless otherwise provided	25
For assignment record, abstract of title and certificate	25
Library service	50
List of U.S. patents and SIRs in subclass	3
Status of maintenance fee payments	10
Copy of non-U.S. documents	25
Comparing and certifying copy	25
Additional filing receipt	25
Filing a disclosure document	10
Local delivery box rental (per annum)	50
International type search report	40
Recording each patent assignment	40
Publication in *Official Gazette*	25
Labor charges for services per hour	30
Retaining abandoned application	130
Handling fee for incomplete or improper application	130
APS-text terminal session time, per hour	40
APS-CSIR terminal session time, per hour	50
Patent coupons	3
Handling fee for withdrawal of SIR	130

Patent Enrollment Fees	
Admission to examination	$ 310
Registration to practice	100
Reinstatement to practice	15
Copy of certificate of good standing	10

Finance Service Fees	
Establish deposit account	$ 10
Service charge for below minimum balance	25
Processing returned checks	50

Keep in mind, these fees are generally less than you may spend for a patent agent or attorney. While fees vary nationwide, you can expect to pay a patent agent $1,000 to $3,500 for preparing your application. Patent attorneys, on the other hand, will charge you anywhere from $3,000 to $10,000 for the same preparation. There are also charges for the actual patent drawings; they range from $75 to $200 per drawing. In some areas, there are patent experts or consultants who will assist you in preparing your own patent application, and will usually charge less than $1,000 for their services.

Be careful to avoid con artists in this profession. It may be wise to avoid the services found in the back of a supermarket tabloid and some of the so-called inventor assistance groups known for their 800 numbers publicized on late-night television. These services may end up costing you a great deal of money and accomplish little. Although it would be unfair to assume that all invention brokers are of questionable character, many are more concerned about profit from inventors than profit from inventions. Use common sense when choosing any business associate.

3

Trademarks, Service Marks, and Copyrights

Doing easily what others find difficult is talent, doing what is impossible for talent is genius. — Henri F. Amiel

Trademarks and Service Marks

If your creation includes any written or artistic matter which includes a symbol, word, shape, or design, and you use this mark as a brand name, service mark, or trade dress, you qualify for protection under trademark law.

Trademarks are used by a manufacturer or merchant both to identify goods, and to distinguish them from those goods manufactured or sold by others. A trademark can be obtained as easily as affixing the letters ™ to your mark, or you can register it with state or federal trademark offices.

Many people consider trademarks a brand name and will buy products based upon their former experiences with a certain trademark. Service marks are sometimes confused with trademarks, but are actually slogans or phrases used in the sale or advertising of services rather than products.

Service marks identify the services of one person or company and distinguish them from the services of others. For example, the use of the slogan, "We print it in a minute" by a printing business indicates the type of services rendered to its customers. Service marks and trademarks are registered in the same way.

A trademark only protects you from someone else's use of a similar mark when its use could cause confusion. A trademark of an anchor for a line of boats could in fact be registered again for a line of clothes.

But if you were selling a line of boats, you could not modify someone's trademark of an anchor and use it yourself.

If a trademark is federally registered in the U.S. Patent and Trademark Office, the ® symbol, or the words, "Registered in the U.S. Patent and Trademark Office" must be used. Failure to give this notice prevents you from recovering damages for trademark infringement. If your trademark or service mark is not registered federally or is registered only in your state, a ™ or ℠ is used to identify this condition. The ™ or ℠ symbol must be smaller than the actual trademark and must follow the mark. Before deciding on a size for your ™ symbol, you may wish to look at other marks found on other goods to get a feel for such things as artwork and the size comparison between the trademark and the symbol.

A trademark is owned by the first person or company to use the mark in commerce, meaning whoever first uses it in public is considered the owner of the mark, whether the mark is registered or not. There are certain conditions which must be met before you can register a trademark. One is that the mark cannot be recorded as belonging to another person or organization. That is why it is advisable when applying for a federal trademark to have a search done, although it is not necessary for state registration.

Another condition is that it must not resemble another mark or be of a content so as to confuse or deceive a buyer. One example of this would be if a trademark said, "China Fashions" and the clothes were designed and manufactured in Oklahoma. The trademark would most likely be refused registration.

This should be considered if you intend to start with a state trademark and later obtain a federal trademark; your marketing power could be damaged by having to change your logo in midstream. After meeting these conditions, a trademark can be obtained and even licensed. Your trademark is intellectual property, and you have the right to use it and even seek protection from the courts if someone else tries to infringe upon it. With your trademark also comes a responsibility to maintain adequate quality control. The value of a trademark is that the public sees it as an exclusive sign of a business, and bad news often travels faster than good news.

In cases where the product is sold directly to the consumer, the trademark is extremely valuable. For example, if you knew the formula for Coca-Cola® and sold it on the market under a different name, many people would say it tasted different, and most Coca-Cola® drinkers would not even try it at all because they have come to rely on certain manufacturers for quality. Once the quality of your product gains a name for itself, others will have the same trouble getting people away from your product to try theirs.

Trademarks should never be underestimated as a marketing tool for product success. Unlike patents, trademarks have an indefinite life when used properly. Federal trademarks are issued for a period of ten years and can be renewed if still in use.

You can, however, lose a trademark by letting it become generic. This is when people begin using your brand name to describe the type of product. For instance, people often say, "xeroxed copies" instead of saying "photocopies." To avoid having your trademark become generic, a trademark should be used as an adjective modifying a noun. An example of this would be "Scotch® Brand Tape" made by the 3M Company. The significance of saying "Brand" here is to show that Scotch is only one of many brands of tape and as such is not a generic name. In calling this same product Scotch Tape, for example, the product becomes generic and the 3M Company could thereby lose its trademark.

Terms that were once trademarks but are now public domain include:

Aspirin	High octane	Nylon
Corn flakes	Kerosene	Raisin bran
Cube steak	Lanolin	Thermos bottle
Dry ice	Linoleum	Trampoline
Escalator	Mimeograph	

All of these trademarks were lost because proper precautions were not taken and the names became generic. Filing a trademark yourself could cost as little as $25 for a state trademark. Although this text has discussed trademarks as they relate to products within the marketplace, there are provisions for reserving a trademark if you are less than six months away froesem the marketplace.

The Trademark Law Revision Act of 1988, Title 1 of Public Law No. 100-667, which went into effect November 16, 1989, allows someone who has a bona fide intent to use the trademark in commerce to apply for federal registration, thus avoiding the need to wait until the trademark is in actual use. However, the trademark should be used in commerce within six months after the date of issuance of the "Notice of Allowance," and a verified statement of its use should be filed with the U.S. Patent and Trademark Office. Other important provisions of the 1988 Revision Act reduced the registration term from 20 to 10 years. The act also subjects anyone who makes a false statement in advertising about his or her own or someone else's goods to liability in a civil action brought by any person injured by such statements.

The Federal Trademark Application

A federal trademark application is comprised of:

- A written application form;
- A drawing of the work;
- Three specimens showing actual use of the mark in connection with the goods or service; and
- The required filing fee.

For general information and the appropriate forms, contact:

Trademark Assistance Center
(703) 308-9000

The written application form must be in English and include a heading to identify the mark, a class number. You must also specify if you are a sole proprietorship, partnership, or corporation and whether you wish to apply on the basis of actual use or intent to use. Send your application to:

Assistant Commissioner for Trademarks
2900 Crystal Drive, Room 10B10
Arlington, VA 22202-3513
(703) 308-8900
FAX (703) 308-7220

If you wish to register a trademark in your state, call or write to your secretary of state for forms and instructions. The cost varies from state to state and can range from $10 to $50.

Federal Trademark Costs

Listed below are some of the costs you may encounter in the federal trademark process.

Trademark Processing Fees

Application for registration, per class	$245
Filing an amendment to allege use under, per class	100
Filing a statement of use under, per class	100
Six-month extension, statement of use	100
Application for renewal, per class	300
Additional fee for late renewal, per class	100
Publication of mark under, per class	100
Issuing new certificate of registration	100
Certificate of correction, registrant's error	100
Filing disclaimer to registration	100
Filing amendment to registration	100
Filing affidavit, per class	100
Petition for cancellation, per class	200
Notice of opposition, per class	200
Ex parte appeal, per class	100
Dividing an application, per new application created	100

Trademark Service Fees

Printed copy of each registered mark, regular service	$ 3
Printer copy of each registered mark, expedited	6
EPO expedited service of registered mark	25
Certified copy of registered mark, regular service	10
Certified copy of registered mark, expedited service	20
Copy of application as filed	15
Copy of application as filed, expedited service	30
Copy of file wrapper and contents	50
Recording trademark assignment	40

What You Cannot Trademark

You cannot trademark these types of material.

- A person's likeness, without that person's consent;
- Descriptive words;
- Generic words;
- Geographical locations;

- Governmental emblems;
- Immoral, scandalous, or deceptive matter;
- Marks that may cause confusion;
- Personal names;
- Slogans; and
- Trade names.

Trademarks as Marketing Tools

Can you imagine going to a store and finding products on the shelves without brand names? The inferior products would look exactly the same as the superior products. It wouldn't be long before the better manufacturers lost all incentive to maintain their high quality standards, because they would not enjoy greater sales for their extra efforts.

Trademarks are an important part of how consumers purchase a product. If you bought a brand-name refrigerator that worked well, you would be more inclined to purchase a stove by the same company, even though they are entirely different products. A company's reputation can make a future product successful simply through its trademark.

Trademark Art

For inventors considering designing their own trademark artwork, consult with a graphic artist or industrial designer familiar with trademark design. A quality trademark will ensure the consumer of a quality product. Your trademark must be well thought out, unique, and, above all, it must be original.

Compulsory Trademark Licensing

By now, you have thought of trademarks that may not follow the established rules. It seems that there are always exceptions to the rules, and one such exception is the trademark, "RealLemon®" owned by the Borden Company. Even though descriptive words cannot be trademarked, occasionally one slips by.

In the case of "RealLemon®," the Borden Company probably wishes it hadn't slipped past. After a lengthy legal hearing by a Federal Trade

Commission administrative law judge, it was decided that Borden would be required to license its trademarks to all its competitors for a very small royalty. This compulsory license is now available to anyone who asks for it. The end result is a trademark which now has little or no meaning, because the company failed to follow some basic rules on what can and cannot be trademarked.

Copyrights

If your written or artistic endeavors include any of the following tangible mediums of expression, you qualify for a copyright. Copyrights offer legal protection just like patents and trademarks, but they are much easier to obtain. As the law defines it today, copyrights protect original works of authorship fixed to any tangible medium of expression, including:

Architectural design	Drama	Pantomimes
Articles	E-mail	Pictorials
Books	Graphics	Poems
Cartoons	Motion pictures	Sculptured works
Choreographic works	Music	Sound recordings
Computer software programs	Paintings	Video recordings

Copyright Law

Copyright law in the United States has its foundation in Article I, Section 8, Clause 8, of the Constitution and is embodied in Title 17, United States Code. Under the Federal Copyright Statutes, which were enacted in 1976 and became effective January 1, 1978, there is no longer any state copyright protection.

The copyright act grants to authors and artists the exclusive right to reproduce, adapt, revise, and translate as well as distribute, sell, display, and license their works. In addition, copyright law grants authors, composers, programmers, artists, and the like, the right to prevent others from copying, using, or selling their original creation without permission.

Copyrights do not give an author rights to the information contained within a book, only the method and style in which the information is presented.

Unlike patents, copyrights are obtained the minute the work assumes some tangible form, and last for 50 years after the creator's death.

Copyright Notice

It is no longer necessary for a copyright notice to be given to the U.S. Copyright Office. Even though it is no longer mandatory, you can still register your work with the U.S. Copyright Office for $20 and give the general public notice of copyright. Because the U.S. Copyright Office receives more than half a million copyright applications annually, a certificate of registration can take up to 16 weeks to receive.

If you do decide to give notice of copyright on your work, the proper way to do this is to write "Copyright," followed by the year the work is completed, followed by your name or company name. You may also use the symbol © for recordings and records as an alternative to writing "Copyright."

A copyright notice looks something like this:

© 1996 Quest International

You may also abbreviate "Copyright" to "Copr." and add the words, "All Rights Reserved" below the copyright notice.

To obtain the best information and registration forms, contact:

U.S. Copyright Office
Washington, DC 20559
(202) 287-9100

Or, you can reach this office via their Internet address:

http://lcweb.loc.gov/copyright/

There may also be a local phone number to call for copyright information; check your telephone directory.

Copyright Protection

The exclusive rights in copyrighted works are set forth in Title 17, United States Code Section 106; these rights, however, are subject to the provisions of Title 17 Sections 107–108. Generally, when you copyright a work you have the following exclusive rights:

- The right to reproduce the copyrighted work in copies or records;
- The right to prepare derivative works based upon the copyrighted work;
- The right to distribute copies or records of the copyrighted work to the public, by sale or other transfer of ownership, or by rental, lease, or lending;
- In the case of literary, musical, dramatic, and choreographic works, pantomimes, motion pictures, and other audio-visual works, the right to publicly perform the copyrighted work; and
- In the case of literary, musical, dramatic, and choreographic works, pantomimes and pictorial, graphic, or cultural works, including the individual images of a motion picture or other audio-visual work, the right to publicly display the copyrighted work.

Ownership of Copyrights

The ownership of a copyright is initially held by the author or authors of the work. When the copyright is prepared under employment or contract, the employer is the owner. In the same way as with patents and trademarks, the exclusive rights comprising in a copyright may be assigned or licensed. When ownership of a copyright is transferred in any way, the author must inform the U.S. Copyright Office within one month after the execution of the transfer for the transfer to be valid.

An advantage to copyrights is their long life, which can in turn increase the royalty life when licensed. Licensing is discussed in Chapter 8.

Mandatory Deposit Requirement

Under the requirements set forth in the United States Copyright Act, all works under copyright protection and published in the United States on or after March 1, 1989 are subject to mandatory deposit whether published with or without copyright notice. These requirements are similar to the "legal deposit" or "deposit legal" laws in effect in other countries.

The mandatory deposit provision ensures that the U.S. Copyright Office is entitled to receive copies of every copyrightable work published in the United States. Section 407 of the copyright act states that these deposits "are available to the Library of Congress for its collections, or for exchange or transfer to any other library."

How the Mandatory Deposit Requirement Works

Section 407 of the copyright law requires the "owner of the copyright or the exclusive right of publication" in a work published in the United States to deposit the required number of copies in the U.S. Copyright Office within three months of the date of such publication.

Publication is defined in the copyright law as "the distribution of copies or phonorecords of a work to the public by sale or other transfer of ownership, or by rental, lease, or lending."

Under Section 407, deposit for the collections of the Library of Congress is mandatory; registration of a copyright claim under Section 408 is voluntary. While not a condition of copyright protection, registration may under certain circumstances allow the owner a broader range of remedies in infringement suits. To satisfy requirements for both, the following must be sent in one package to the register of copyrights:

- Mandatory deposit copies;
- A completed application for registration; and
- A $20 nonrefundable filing fee payable to the register of copyrights.

Deposits should be sent to:

Register of Copyrights
Attn. 407 Deposits
Library of Congress
Washington, DC 20559-6000

Derivative Works

Copyright law also allows for derivative work — for example, a work that is based on, or derived from, one or more already existing works is copyrightable if it includes what the copyright law calls an "original work of authorship." A new version, which may include translations, musical arrangements, dramatization, fictionalizations, art reproductions, and condensations, must be different enough from the original to be regarded as a "new work" or must contain a substantial amount of new material. The new material must be original and copyrightable in itself.

A typical example of a derivative work received for registration in the U.S. Copyright Office is something that is primarily a new work but incorporates some previously published material. This previously pu lished material makes the work a derivative work under the copyrigh. law. However, if information is simply to be transformed, wherein the information you are currently reading has been taken from existing copyright enclosures, that would not be considered a derivative work.

Examples of derivative works would include a television drama based on a novel; a motion picture based on a play; a novel in English that is translated from a book originally published in Russian; a drawing based on a photograph; or even a sculpture based on a drawing.

Although not required by law, it is perfectly acceptable for a work to contain a notice for the original material, as well as for the new work. For example, if a previously registered book contains only a new introduction, the notice might be:

© 1937 John Doe; introduction © 1996 Dale Davis

Internet Access to Copyright Information

U.S. Copyright Office publications, circulars, announcements, and regulations are now available on the Internet and may be examined and downloaded through the Library of Congress. To connect through the Library of Congress Gopher, LC MARVEL, do the following:

Telnet

marvel.loc.gov

Log in as "marvel" to access the system. Then, select the Copyright menu.

Gopher

marvel.loc.gov, port 70

World Wide Web

http://lcweb.loc.gov/copyright

Access to LC MARVEL may be gained through the World Wide Web (WWW). Connections to the WWW resources are made by specifying a Uniform Resource Location (URL) through your client software. The WWW address gives you access to information created by the U.S. Copyright Office and links you to other copyright resources created elsewhere.

A glossary of on-line terms and acronyms is provided at the end of this chapter.

Copyright Office Files Now Available

U.S. Copyright Office Records in machine-readable form cataloged from January 1, 1978 to the present, including registration information and recorded documents, are now available over the Internet. These include the following file names:

- COHM, which contains all original and renewal registrations except serials;
- COHD, which contain documents; and
- COHS, which contains serials.

These files may be examined through the Library of Congress Information System (LOCIS). You can connect to LOCIS directly by using Telnet, or you can also reach LOCIS through the Library of Congress Gopher, LC MARVEL and the WWW.

To connect to LOCIS, do the following:

Telnet

locis.loc.gov or to the numeric address 140.147.254.3 or:
Marvel.loc.gov or to the numeric address 140.147.248.7

Log in as "marvel" to access the system. Then, select the Copyright menu.

Gopher

marvel.loc.gov, port 70

World Wide Web

http://lcweb.loc.gov/copyright

Access Times

LC MARVEL and the WWW are available 24 hours a day. LOCIS is available Eastern time Monday–Friday, 6:30 A.M.–9:30 P.M.; Saturday, 8 A.M.–5 P.M.; Sunday, 1 P.M.–5 P.M. LOCIS is unavailable on all federal holidays.

Cost

The best news of all is that the Library of Congress and the U.S. Copyright Office charge no fees to connect to their Internet resources. The only fees you will pay are to your Internet provider.

Other On-line Sources

In addition to the U.S. Copyright Office on-line resources, you can access some of the following sources electronically to find out more on copyright and intellectual property law.

Copyright Act of 1976

http://www.law.cornell.edu/usc/17/overview.html

This act sets forth the basic rules of copyright, including the 1994 Chip Protection Act. This access also permits full text searches of the law.

Copyright Clearance Center On-line

http://www.copyright.com

This is a non-profit information service group.

Digital Future Coalition

http://home.worldwide.net/dfc

This site provides information from a coalition opposed to pending copyright legislation.

Intellectual Property and the National Information Infrastructure White Paper

http://www.uspto.gov/text/pto/nii/ipwg.html

This site includes copy of pending legislation to amend U.S. Copyright Act.

Software Publishers Assoc.

http://www.spa.org

Trade group that supports pending legislation to strengthen U.S. copyright law.

Ten Big Myths About Copyright

http://www.clari.net/brad/copymyths.html

This is an electronic newspaper.

Trade Secrets

To qualify for a trade secret, you must have information that is not known by the public and which gives you or your company an advantage. Trade secrets include techniques, designs, materials, processes, and formulas. If you have an idea or information you wish to keep secret, you would qualify for trade secret protection. Trade secrets can be licensed the same way as a patent.

The concept of the trade secret was developed by the judicial system to protect formulas and other manufacturing secrets. In contrast to patents, which usually last 17 years, a trade secret lasts as long as you can keep it a secret. Patents also require a disclosure of the formulas and technologies involved, which can be duplicated. Of course, trade secrets are not as easy to duplicate because they are kept secret.

The most famous example of a trade secret is the formula for Coca-Cola®. The basic ingredients are readily identified as water, sugar, caramel coloring, and carbonation; however, the exact quantities and cooking process are shrouded in mystery and locked away in a high security vault. If patented, the formula would be made public, and anyone could send for a copy of the patent, and even try to modify and improve it. The Coca-Cola® formula has remained a trade secret years after an actual patent would have expired.

An idea need not be patentable in order to receive trade secret protection, nor is novelty a requirement. Trade secrets can cover the entire range of business practices. The Uniform Trade Secrets Act safeguards trade secrets if three conditions are met.

- The trade secret must have economic value. This can be any proprietary information including formulas, techniques, pricing information, sales forecasts, and customer information which would give another person or company a competitive advantage.
- Trade secrets must be secret or unknown to the public and difficult to uncover.
- The owner of a trade secret must attempt to protect it. If you have employees, they must be made aware of its secrecy. Furthermore, any visiting sales representatives, vendors, customers, inspectors, or the like must be informed of its secrecy if they must have access to such information. This is usually the hardest requirement in ensuring secrecy.

You might consider a confidentiality or nondisclosure agreement. The best confidentiality or nondisclosure agreements are phrased so as not to define exactly what you consider to be the company's trade secrets.

The definition of your company's proprietary information must be broad enough to cover future advances in technology. The document should contain language strong enough to show a court that you consider your trade secret a vital part of your business and that monetary damages should be in order. Preparing a strong document now could help you avoid a court case later. An additional method of protecting your trade secret is stamping all relevant information "confidential." This can also help courts determine whether or not information was treated as a trade secret. If you feel as though you have competitors who would actually go through your trash, consider getting a shredding machine.

Before you go to court to sue a competitor, remember two things. First, a trade secret court case is usually expensive and can take years to resolve. Second, another competitor can sit in on a public hearing and listen to you tell the court your trade secret.

Unfair Competition

Unfair competition is a very broad term defining legal standards of business conduct. It provides protection against such things as simulation of trade packaging, using similar corporate and professional names, misappropriation of trade secrets, and palming off one person's goods as those of another. Many inventors sometimes impressed by a big-name product have a tendency to follow another company's trade dress.

Unfair competition law can be utilized, with or without other forms of protection, to protect your trade dress. For example, if you were selling your unprotected product packaged in a bright-green box with stars on it, and a competitor tried to cash in on your marketing success by using a bright-green box with stars on it, you could stop your competitor by using unfair competition law. The same would apply if a competitor used a similar name, such as changing "Starclips" to "Starclippers." Again, using unfair competition law, you could sue any competitor for using similar trade dress.

If your product should too closely resemble another trade dress, you could find an injunction placed against you, prohibiting you from any further activity in the marketplace until a court decides on your guilt or innocence. If found guilty of unfair competition, a judge would award the damaged company compensation in monetary damages for adding to the public's confusion. There are better ways to spend your profits.

Glossary of On-line Acronyms and Terms

Many people are already very familiar with most of the on-line jargon and terminology, but for those who may not be as familiar with this emerging lingo, here is a brief glossary of on-line acronyms and terms that you may find helpful.

Archie. This is a powerful Internet search tool that will search hundreds of locations for a specific file in the public domain. A similar service called *Veronica* works with gophers.

ARPANET or Advanced Research Projects Agency Network. This is a network sponsored by the Advanced Research Projects Agency, which served as a testbed for many of the communications protocols used in today's Internet.

ASCII or American Standard Code for Information Interchange. This is a method of representing the alphabetic, numeric, and control characters used in computer communications and coded in hexadecimal notation. "ASCII file" is used to indicate a file that is stored in plain text, that is, readable by humans.

BBS or bulletin board system. A BBS is a computer and associated software that typically provides electronic messaging services, archives of files, and any other services or activities of interest to the bulletin board system's operator (SYSOP). Although BBSs have traditionally been the domain of hobbyists, an increasing number of BBSs are connected directly to the Internet, and many BBSs are currently operated by government, educational, and research institutions.

Cyberspace. This represents almost anyplace computer users are on-line.

FAQ or frequently asked questions. This is a file maintained by most newsgroups that answer questions all newbies seem to ask.

Flame wars. These are heated debates via electronic messages.

FTP or file transfer protocol. It is a machine and operating system independent method of transferring files between computers connected to the Internet.

Gopher. A document delivery system that allows information from all over the Internet to be presented to a user in a hierarchically organized front end. Gopher users can search through remote documents for texts of interest and can retrieve remote documents to their local systems.

Hacker. This refers to someone who is highly computer-literate. It can also refer to someone who breaks into computers and networks, although some suggest the name "cracker."

IAP or Internet access provider. A company — there are hundreds across the U.S. — that provides an e-mail address and/or access to the Internet by modem via local phone lines.

IRQ or Interrupt ReQuest. An internal computer language for communicating with hardware, giving each device an address to avoid conflicting internal processing of two devices at the same time.

JPL or Jet Propulsion Laboratory. A government owned research laboratory operated for NASA by the California Institute of Technology.

Kb or kilobyte. 1024 bytes — a byte is a storage location that is typically used to store a letter or a number.

Kb/sec. or kilobytes per second. The most common measure of the rate at which data is transferred.

LAN or local area network. A network connecting computers in a relatively small area, usually within a room, building, or set of buildings.

LISTSERV. This is a software program for efficient setup and maintenance of discussion groups. LISTSERV groups can be subscribed to by Internet users and many LISTSERV discussion groups are gatewayed to USENET newsgroups.

Mb or megabyte. One million bytes of storage. The amount of information stored in a file or on a disk is usually identified in megabytes or kilobytes.

Mosaic. A WWW server application available free of charge from NCSA.

NCSA. An acronym for the National Center for Supercomputing Applications in Champaign, Illinois.

Newbies. A derisive term used by Internet veterans to describe people who are still getting their feet wet on the "Net."

Newsgroup. A topical discussion group within USENET propagated via newsfeeds to a loosely defined, worldwide network of computers, including many on the Internet. One may submit messages to a newsgroup and read other messages with newsreader software.

Packet switching. The process of routing and transferring data by way of electronic signals.

SLIP or serial line Internet protocol. A communications protocol used over serial lines — such as computers connected via modem to dial-up phone circuits — to support Internet protocol (IP) connectively.

SYSOPS or systems operators. The person responsible for the day-to-day maintenance of an Internet host; sometimes abbreviated as "sysadmin" or "admin." Usually, a SYSOP works for an institution and does not technically "own" the host, but nonetheless is vested with responsibilities and privileges associated with ownership.

TCP/IP or transmission control protocol over Internet protocol. A set of protocols that make Telnet, FTP, electronic mail, and other services possible among the computers within a heterogeneous network.

TELENET. Not to be confused with Telnet! A commercial e-mail service, packet-switched network using the CCITT X.25 protocols.

Telnet. The Internet standard protocol allowing log-ins to remote hosts. With Telnet, one has access to the commands, services, and central processing unit of the remote host.

USENET. A collection of thousands of topically named newsgroups, the set of computers that exchange some or all of these newsgroups, and the community of people who read or submit USENET news. Not all Internet hosts subscribe to USENET newsgroups, and USENET newsgroups may be received by non-Internet hosts.

WAIS or wide area information server. A client-server information service system based on the Z39.50 protocol which allows users to search through heterogeneous databases with a single user interface.

WWW or world wide web. A client-server software package that uses hypertext to organize and present information services throughout the Internet.

4

Research Your Idea

The way I see it, if you want the rainbow, you gotta put up with the rain. — Dolly Parton

Why Research?

When people think of an inventor, they often conjure up images of an absent-minded, wild-haired professor, working in a laboratory filled with bubbling test tubes and elaborate electronic machines, or at a blackboard filled with intricate mathematical calculations. To many people, an inventor is a strange combination of scientist and dreamer, but people rarely consider her an expert. In fact, most inventors really are experts in their own fields.

Researching your invention is a sound investment that will affect every stage of your product development. Just as a patent search will inform you of your chances for gaining a patent, the general research you do will assist you in the development and marketing of your product. For example, research can assist you in finding similar products or parts to make your product. It can teach you new processes or even where to market. In short, research can help you learn almost everything regarding your invention, its industry, and its marketplace.

Research may not seem all that thrilling at times, but it is an important way of strengthening your armor when being questioned by a potential licensee. When it comes time to license or market your invention, any lack of knowledge will become apparent. A little research now can help you avoid an "I don't know" later. Information will also help you compete. Without it, your potential is limited. One inventor recently asked a consultant for information on how to sell some jewelry she had invented. The consultant referred to the *Directory of Conventions* — which is available at most libraries — and showed her a list of jewelry trade shows that are held throughout the United States. She then looked in the library phone books for other wholesalers in areas such as Los Angeles and New York. Not having this information was holding her back; a little research opened the gates to success. If your invention fails for lack of information, you have no one to blame but yourself.

Libraries Are a Great Place to Start

Library-user studies show that only between 10 and 20 percent of adults account for 90 to 95 percent of all books borrowed from U.S. libraries. This lack of use by adults may help explain why so many new businesses fail. To succeed, you need to know about your product's consumer, its industry, and its competition. Keep this in mind, and plan a trip to your local library.

Consider your time spent at the library as an investment in your invention. The mere thought of paying a researcher $25 to $50 an hour can make that task easier to swallow. In general, the library is always the best first stop when doing any kind of research. All libraries offer great riches if you remember some basic guidelines.

- Remember that libraries work in systems. No library has everything, but collectively, they offer endless possibilities.
- Don't judge a library by its size. All libraries have something to offer, including the services of a librarian.
- Remember that when working with librarians, your right to confidentiality is assured.
- Libraries offer professional guidance and will assist you in a variety of search strategies.
- Take the time to browse, especially in the reference sections.

There are several types of libraries you may be able to visit besides your local city library. Depending on your location, you could tap the resources of an academic, company, newspaper, or special library.

Academic Libraries

University and college libraries serve the research needs of scholars, students, and researchers, and they have a large number of professional-level books. While many libraries limit their use to faculty and students, most will allow one-time or occasional visits or allow you to buy a membership.

Company Libraries

Large companies — such as the Automobile Club of Southern California, Twentieth Century-Fox motion picture studio, Hallmark Cards, Inc., and the Pillsbury Company — have extensive libraries, generally to help their employees perform their duties more efficiently. There may be a large company near you that can help you in your research.

Newspaper Libraries

Many large newspaper libraries have reference book and magazine collections for their staff to use in verifying information, and they have been known to allow others to use these resources. Check with the newspaper's editor or publisher.

Special Libraries

The directories listed below identify libraries of every kind and can direct you in any research endeavor. The best place to locate these directories is — you guessed it — your local library.

- *American Library Directory*. This directory, published by the R.R. Bowker Company, lists more than 30,000 U.S. and Canadian libraries from hospital to zoo libraries.
- *Directory of Special Libraries and Information Centers*. Published by Gale Research, Inc., this directory features five volumes of special libraries.
- *Research Centers Directory*. Published by Gale Research, Inc., this directory lists nongovernmental research centers.
- *Subject Collection*. Published by the R.R. Bowker Company, this directory lists 7,000 academic, public, museum, and historical society libraries nationwide.

Other Research Sources

In addition to libraries, you have a number of other resources that you can use to research your idea or invention and to market it more thoroughly.

You can also access valuable information through various directories, databases, Small Business Institutes, and industrial application centers.

Directories

Directories can not only refer you to other special libraries — as listed above — but they can also provide you with pertinent and timely information on new product development, inventor news, industry trends, and manufacturers, to name a few. Below, you will find several of these types of directories listed. These directories are generally available at most libraries.

Inventor Directories

- *Directory of Corporate Affiliations*
- *Dun & Bradstreet Million Dollar Directory*
- *Dun's Industrial Guide*
- *Standard & Poor Register of Corporations*
- *Standard Directory of Advertisers*

Current Business Information Directories

- *Business Index*
- *Business Periodicals Index*
- *County and City Data Book*
- *Encyclopedia of Business Information Sources*
- *F&S Index*
- *Index to How-To-Do-It Information*
- *Moody's Investor's Industry Review*
- *Oil Industry Comparative Appraisals*
- *Predicast*
- *Standard & Poor's Industry Surveys*
- *U.S. Industrial Outlook*
- *The Wall Street Journal/Barron's Index*

International Directories

- *Dun & Bradstreet Principal International Businesses*
- *International Directory of Corporate Affiliations*

Manufacturers' Directories

- *10-K Report*
- *Annual Reports*
- *Kelly's Manufacturers and Merchants Directory*
- *MacRae's Blue Book*
- *Moody's Manuals*
- *Standard & Poor's Corporation Records*
- *State Directories*
- *Thomas Register*
- *U.S. Industrial Directory*

Government Publications

- *Attorneys and Agents Registered to Practice before the U.S. Patent & Trademark Office* (patent office booklet)
- *Classification Definition* (patent office booklet)
- *General Information Concerning Patents* (patent office booklet)
- *Index to the U.S. Patent Classification* (patent office booklet)
- *Manual of Classification* (patent office booklet)
- *Official Gazette* (patent office publication)
- *Survey of Current Business* (U.S. Department of Commerce)

Databases

In today's ever-increasing on-line world of information, you have tremendous opportunities to gather information related to your project or invention through the Information Super Highway's databases and public information. The databases listed below can provide valuable demographic, new product, and industry information. Don't forget to tap government on-line services for additional information. The more information you gather, the better educated you will be on your product's viability.

CompuServe
5000 Arlington Centre Blvd.
P.O. Box 20212
Columbus, OH 43220
(800) 848-8199 (Nationwide)

A business database that offers more than 450 publications.

DataTimes
14000 Quail Springs Parkway, Suite 450
Oklahoma City, OK 73134
(800) 642-2525 (Nationwide)

This service provides access to 1,200 test sources, including 118 newspapers and 20 financial files.

Delphi/General Videotex Corp.
1030 Massachusetts Avenue, 4th Floor
Cambridge, MA 02138
(800) 695-4005 (Nationwide)

This database offers more than 150 information and communication services.

Dialog/Data-Star
One Commerce Square, Suite 1010
Philadelphia, PA 19103
(800) 221-7754 (Nationwide)

This database provides access to more than 300 databases that offer international information to businesses.

Dow Jones News/Retrieval
P.O. Box 300
Princeton, NJ 08543-0300
(609) 452-1511

This database features news articles of *The Wall Street Journal* since 1979.

Genie
401 North Washington Street
Rockville, MD 20850
(800) 638-9636 (Nationwide)

Genie offers more than 100 services, including Dun & Bradstreet reports.

Newsnet, Inc.
945 Haverford Road
Bryn Mawr, PA 19010
(800) 345-1301 (Nationwide)

This database has access to business news from more than 675 newsletters and wire services covering 35 industries.

ORBIT Search Service
8000 Westpark Drive
McLean, VA 22102
(800) 456-7248 (Nationwide)

This service has access to more than 120 databases dealing with scientific and technical issues.

Small Business Institutes

Small Business Institutes (SBIs), organized through the U.S. Small Business Administration (SBA), are found at almost 500 university and college campuses nationwide. At each SBI, senior and graduate students in the school of business administration and faculty advisers provide on-site management counseling and an in-depth analysis of a firm's business situation. Students are guided by the faculty advisers and SBA management assistance experts, and receive academic credits for their research work. This can be a great help for those in-depth research projects. To see if there is an SBI near you, contact your local SBA office.

Industrial Application Centers

Industrial application centers serve as technology utilization resources nationwide for industrial firms, individuals, agencies, public and private organizations, faculty and student personnel, and institutions concerned with the promotion of economic and technological developments. The main purpose of these centers is to help users of new technology obtain information appropriate to their needs.

Industrial application centers administer technology transfer through the National Aeronautics & Space Administration's (NASA's) Technology Transfer Program. The technology available for transfer was all made through development programs of NASA and is available for national use. For a nominal fee, or sometimes even at no cost, the centers will tie into the extensive NASA database, allowing you access to literally millions of documents from worldwide sources.

Industrial application centers are generally associated with universities; they can also be located by contacting a chamber of commerce or your local library. You can obtain more information about these services by calling or writing the nearest industrial application center. This list can help you locate the center nearest you.

Central Industrial Application Center – CIAC
National Aeronautics & Space Administration – NASA
P.O. Box 1335
Durant, OK 74702
(405) 924-5094
(800) 658-2823 (Nationwide)

Indianapolis Center for Advanced Research – ICAR
611 North Capitol Avenue
Indianapolis, IN 46204
(317) 262-5036

Industrial Application Center – IAC
Southern University – NASA
Department of Computer Science
P.O. Box 9737
Baton Rouge, LA 70813-9737
(504) 771-6272
(504) 771-4950

Industrial Application Center – IAC
University of Pittsburgh – NASA
823 William Pitt Union
Pittsburgh, PA 15260
(412) 648-7000

Industrial Application Center – IAC
University of Southern California – NASA
Research Annex, 3716 South Hope Street
Los Angeles, CA 90007-4344
(213) 743-6132
(800) 642-2872 (California only)
(800) 872-7477 (Nationwide)

NERAC, Inc.
One Technology Drive
Tolland, CT 06084
(203) 872-7000

Science and Technology Research Center – STRC
Research Triangle Park
P.O. Box 12235
Durham, NC 27709-2235
(919) 549-0671

Southern Technology Application Center – STAC
Progress Center
One Progress Blvd., Box 24
Alachua, FL 32615
(904) 462-3913
(800) 354-4832 (Florida only)
(800) 225-0308 (Nationwide)

Technology Application Center – TAC
University of New Mexico
Albuquerque, NM 87131
(505) 277-3622

Technology Application Program – TAP
University of Kentucky – NASA
109 Kinkead Hall
Lexington, KY 40506-0057
(606) 257-6322

One source you may find particularly helpful in locating industrial application centers is the NASA/Small Business Innovation Research (SBIR) Electronic Bulletin Board System (BBS). This BBS provides dial-in access for downloading solicitation and other NASA/SBIR information. It operates up to 9,600 baud, no parity, 8 data bits, and 1 stop bit. The caller's terminal type should be set to ANSI or VT-100.

NASA/SBIR Electronic BBS
(202) 488-2939 (Washington, DC)
(800) 547-1811 (Nationwide)

Notes

5

Create Your Prototype

Invention is a combination of brains and material. The more brains you use, the less material you need. — Charles F. Kettering

Turn Ideas into Reality

An idea is just an idea until it takes some tangible form. To add credibility and value to your idea, you must have a prototype. The prototype of your invention will do more than just prove that the idea works. It will also:

- Test the materials selection and the manufacturing process you intend to use;
- Generate important data concerning time requirements, processes, and labor; and
- Solve unforeseen problems.

Most importantly, it will turn your intangible idea into something tangible, a real invention.

Your prototype may be difficult to create because of your lack of knowledge on processes or the difficulty in obtaining materials, but trying to sell an invention without a prototype can be similar to trying to sell the London Bridge without a deed. When you begin to develop your prototype, you will also discover the product evolves as it becomes more suitable for production. You can expect your invention to change as it becomes more tangible. There may be minor changes, such as a material change, for instance, changing from polypropylene to nylon, or an even more apparent change where a design is modified to provide for improved manufacturing. Regardless, this time of development will offer you a great opportunity to evaluate your invention.

Be flexible and innovative in solving the problems that will become apparent as your idea starts to take shape. Building the prototype is part of being an inventor, so don't worry if you are not an engineer, mechanic, designer, or model maker. As the inventor, you are the one best qualified to build your invention. You see it in your mind and you know what you want. You are the source of the creativity that brought the idea to life. You should then be the one to make it become a reality.

First prototypes may be built of clay, wood, wire, or any usable material. Even the prototype of the car you now drive was made of clay so that the engineers could see any design mistakes and make improvements.The prototype will also bring to light problems that may surface in manufacturing your invention, making it easier to solve those problems before actual production starts.

Use the experience of building your prototype to have some fun. Be creative in the ways you might build your invention. In one situation, an inventor came up with a very good idea, but it was too expensive for the market because a remote control device was needed for its operation. By not looking at industry to supply the remote control, but a toy store, the inventor was able to reduce the part's cost from about $200 to $3. In creating your prototype, it pays to look around and mix industries. Spend as much time as possible browsing through the aisles of different stores. By doing so, you will discover that parts you find in one industry sometimes work in other industries. Try to catalog your unusual finds for later use; you never know when this kind of research will pay off.

For example, while working on a Small Business Innovation Research (SBIR) project through the U.S. Air Force, an inventor needed an inexpensive fire sprinkler nozzle for chemical dispersal. While the fire protection industry had the needed nozzles, they cost $20 to $30. Because of his past research of other industries, he remembered plastic irrigation nozzles at the garden supply store that would do basically the same thing, and which sold for 30 cents each. Not only did he save money and provide better marketing potential, soon after, he developed a plastic nozzle for the fire protection industry.

Sometimes, a prototype will need to be redesigned in order to utilize existing or readily available parts, so don't be discouraged if you find yourself going back to the drawing board many times. That is a very important part of the prototype experience, and it will often improve your invention.

Depending upon your situation, you may be entitled to certain tax benefits regarding your prototype expenses. You should, therefore, keep all receipts for your prototype development. However, due to the complexity of tax laws and the many factors which must be considered in determining whether your expenses are deductible, contact your tax planner for advice.

Use Efficient Designs

Prototypes usually have one thing in common: they can be expensive to build and rarely lend themselves to mass production. Although your first prototype is usually dedicated to making your invention workable, you should note any improvements that will help you develop a more efficient design. Making the prototype of your invention should occur early in the process of bringing your idea to the marketplace so you can develop and fine-tune the best possible design before incurring costly changes or modifications once production has begun.

The prototype of your invention should serve as an evaluation process in developing a more efficient design. Efficient design may mean discovering labor-saving steps, removing or redesigning parts difficult to assemble, and basically streamlining the process of building your invention. With these improvements, your invention becomes more suitable to manufacturing and marketing and more valuable in contract negotiating as well. Removing unnecessary processes or steps early on reduces the cost, which later will add to your profits and sales success.

All too often people do not take the proper approaches to even the simplest problems. Many inventors suffer from the I-can't-see-the-forest-for-the-trees syndrome. There are many methods for solving a problem, and the method is never as important as the solution. Inventors especially have a tendency to become protective about their ideas. The same determination that makes inventors will at times hinder them in finding solutions to getting their product to market. To demonstrate the importance of looking at a problem from a different angle, look at some of the companies using design efficiency programs today.

For instance, NCR Corporation recently produced a cash register terminal that had 15 parts and could be snapped together in less than two minutes by someone wearing a blindfold. Compared to their old unit, this new terminal reduced assembly time by 75 percent and reduced the number of parts by 80 percent. Fewer parts and less assembly time also reduced testing and packaging, resulting in an estimated $1.1 million savings because of reduced manufacturing costs.

In addition, IBM Corporation redesigned its Proprinter® several years ago; it can now be assembled in only three minutes with 79 percent fewer parts than its predecessor. Ford used more efficient manufacturing and assembly methods when redesigning the new Taurus and achieved an estimated $1 billion in savings.

Optimum Design for Manufacturing and Assembly

Entering the world of manufacturing and marketing has always had its hurdles, but the 21st century will require even more expertise and knowledge to overcome these obstacles because of emerging new and advanced technologies.

For example, Russia, with its emerging market-run economy, is inspiring new product development and technology that will eventually begin to impact the current world marketplace. Many of the liberated Eastern-Bloc countries — as well as many developing Third World countries — are also becoming influences in the worldwide marketplace with new ideas and new technology. While it is exciting to see the results of these new capitalistic economies, the United States needs to be even more prepared to meet the demands of competing in this evolving worldwide market. It is imperative to understand the many new methodologies and processes being developed to assist U.S. firms in being competitive.

Regaining the Competitive Edge

According to a report given to the U.S. House of Representatives on October 19, 1988, by the Congressional Committee on Science, Space, and Technology, the United States is losing more than $340 million a day in trade to foreign competitors. It stated that if trade is to be brought back into balance, Americans will have to produce more products at home and will have to sell more here and abroad. U.S. firms, said the report, are not able to take technology and use it to produce high-quality products in the short time periods that Japanese firms can.

The report further stated that the greatest challenge with respect to America's international competitiveness lies in the education and training of its people. Particular emphasis is needed on technical expertise directly related to product and manufacturing processes.

In the United States, good design involves more than a drawing by which to assemble parts. Product design, or industrial design, involves much more than simply building a product. Today's inventor or industrial designer must take into account such matters as product liability risk, feasibility studies, model making, and accelerated life testing.

Today, product designers must implement cost reductions by the simplification of a design and determine methods of measuring how efficient a design is, in terms of assembly. It has long been recognized that by reducing the number of parts within a design, you will benefit from several advantages, one of which is reduced cost. Fewer parts also add to the quality of a product by removing possible weak links and thereby decreasing maintenance problems; the remaining parts must then be easy to manufacture and assemble.

Because inventors usually build prototypes early in the development of their product, their consideration is generally based on getting the idea or product to work. Most products are never really designed for considerations of manufacturing. Industry has learned that a formalized step-by-step process to analyze a product promotes better design. Given this systematic approach, the inventor or designer of a new product can evaluate and analyze, within its design stages, a competitive product.

Studies have determined that as much as 85 percent of the cost can be designed out of a product, while still in the development stage. The inventor, as a product designer, must be aware of the nature of the different assembly processes and must understand why one process may be more efficient than another. If you are unable to give a sound reason for using a certain process, you may not be as familiar with it as you need to be and may be unaware of other, more efficient procedures that could reduce cost and improve quality.

A product designer must have a sound reason for requiring separate parts that increase assembly time and material cost. Ask yourself if several parts can be combined into one manufactured item. Any combination of parts will eliminate at least one operation in assembly; the combination of parts will further enhance quality, performance, and maintenance.

Some companies use a production engineering methodology that dictates that an engineer avoid complicated or difficult features, but the outcome can often be a large number of simple parts with a high assembly cost and poor reliability. This may be a reasonable alternative only if assembly labor costs are extremely low.

In many cases, the product designer has no knowledge of machine operation cost, process cost, how the design affects assembly, and why many processes are used. An example of this is today's automobile, which can have as many as 20 different kinds of plastics and dozens of different fastener types, all requiring separate tools.

Optimum Design Process

Optimum design can be many things to the people working within different areas of production. Some of the most common definitions state that optimum design is:

- A method for evaluating and reducing manufacturing cost of a product during conceptual stages of product development;
- A method of obtaining more efficient assembly procedures;
- A method of anticipating future problems in manufacturing;
- Simultaneous or concurrent engineering;
- A method to improve quality by making the product simpler;
- A communication tool (communications with manufacturing to understand problems and adjust accordingly); or
- A procedure that considers production factors at the design stage.

Importance of Optimum Design

You have several good reasons for using optimum design as the means for considering factors and variables.

- Optimum design improves product cost, reliability, productivity, and competitiveness. It also reduces inventory and paperwork.
- After manufacturing starts on a product, there are substantial costs for improvements.
- Research shows that 70 to 80 percent of a product's cost is determined in the first 5 percent of its design life.
- Once the initial design is set, few people go back and develop a totally new concept; most changes are merely modifications.

- In many products, fasteners outnumber functional parts, representing a major portion of assembly time.
- Designing for productivity saves dollars which can be utilized toward marketing success.
- A screw may be an easy way to hold two assemblies together, but a snap-fit can eliminate screws and reduce assembly cost.

Some of the contributing factors related to design include cost accounting, direct labor administration, equipment depreciation, insurance, energy, engineering changes, production maintenance, material handling, quality control, inspection, purchasing, receiving, planning, documentation, inventory, and distribution. Optimum design will assist in the development of a quality product by allowing for fewer processing steps, adjustments, mating parts, tolerance stack-up problems, operator frustrations, material control problems, and assembly fixtures.

Rules for Optimum Design

By using the best design, overhead costs relating to the product are reduced. Here are some helpful rules to guide you:

Reduce the number of parts. Eliminating parts or reducing the number of different types of parts can have many benefits, including decreased material, assembly, and tool costs; improved product quality; and reduction in overhead costs because of less documentation, small inventories, fewer suppliers and inspections, simplified production control, and less rework.

Strive to eliminate adjustments. Parts should be designed so that mating surfaces fall into place easily. This can be accomplished by using tapers, chamfers, or aligning features. Part functions should be incorporated; functions should be moved closer together to facilitate less linkage and reduce the need for adjustments; and when possible, electronic correction should be used as a substitute for mechanical alignment. Alignment features can be costly, but the added cost is usually offset by a reduction in assembly time. Parts that are not self-securing should be located immediately on assembly. Avoid the need for clamps. Ensure that parts are located before they are released. Use pilot point screws to avoid cross-threading problems.

Consider access and visibility for each operation. Restricted vision and access can make a simple operation a difficult one; always consider clearance for hands and tools. Parts that ordinarily are easy to assemble can have difficulties due to handling or separating them in bulk. To avoid handling difficulties, include features to prevent nesting (intertwining or locking together). To ensure nontangling, always specify closed-end or compression coil springs. Include safe-holding features for parts with sharp edges. Avoid parts, such as E-clips and snap rings, which require special tools.

Design parts to be easily installed. Eliminate situations where a part can be installed incorrectly. Provide some type of obstruction that will prohibit incorrect assembly and make parts symmetrical so that assembly orientation is not difficult. Use arrows or matching lines for quick alignment of parts which require orientation.

Maximize part symmetry. The more symmetrical a part is, the quicker it can be oriented during the handling phase of assembly. Parts to avoid are those with only a slight asymmetry. If the functional features cannot be made clearly asymmetrical, a clearly visible nonfunctional feature should be added to define the orientation.

To test your product for optimum design, consider these guidelines.

- Test the need for each part's existence as a separate piece. Is there a requirement during assembly or operation that demands separate materials or movement?
- Use integral-locking features, such as captured washers, to reduce assembly time.
- Move the functional components into proximity with one another to reduce connecting cables, linkages, or wires.
- Use multifunctional parts if possible.
- Use off-the-shelf items only when they meet your requirements exactly.

Developing your invention with optimum design in mind will assist you in making production planning that much easier.

Production Planning

Production planning may be a term you have heard in industry and felt it applied only to planners in large companies who make sure materials, resources, assembly labor, and equipment are ready as needed. The fact is, smaller companies require planned production even more than larger companies because of the vulnerability of smaller operations relying on sole-source suppliers. If your product depends on a certain part and that part becomes unavailable, what are your options? Many times, you will have to speculate on production needs. Your marketing plan will, of course, help in these matters, but consumer response will ultimately be the deciding factor.

Many new ventures use manual labor, based upon the assumption that it is the least expensive form of labor, although in some cases, this is not true. Poor production and not being able to respond to the demand of an increasing market can cost you both sales and profits.

Taking into account production volume, number of parts within the assembly, and most methods of assembly, the designer may discover robot or special-purpose transfer assembly machines are best suited from the beginning. If you are in a situation where you feel limited production will soon become high production, high-speed automatic assembly would be a better investment in product competitiveness, even with amortization and higher product cost at first. Your situation may even require contract or private-label assembly until volumes reach the appropriate or desired level.

Deciding the magic number in production requires an understanding of payback schedules and cost data. Finding the proper volumes for payback of automatic assembly, however, can make the difference in whether your product can remain competitive as volumes increase.

Procedures Analysis

To analyze your design and identify features resulting in high-assembly costs, follow these steps.

- Obtain the best information about the product or assembly. Useful items include engineering drawings, exploded three-dimensional views, an existing version of the product, or a prototype.
- Take the assembly apart (or imagine how this might be done).
- Reassemble the product one piece at a time, looking for problem areas.

If you have sufficient information to consider high production, become familiar with the high-speed or robotic tools available for your industry and include these considerations within the analysis. In your analysis, consider whether parts are added one at a time during assembly. This would be the case for some assembly lines where workers add only one part at each station. However, for bench assembly and on many other assembly lines, the workers will often handle two parts simultaneously. Consider if the parts are presented in bulk and randomly oriented, or available in magazines or special containers.

Performing this analysis provides useful information that can result in a reduction in parts and assembly time.

Design for High-Speed and Robot Assembly

The most important and difficult consideration for high-speed automatic assembly or robot assembly is the efficiency with which the individual parts can be handled automatically. In many cases, the basis for cost comparisons will require expert redesign; yet, for the production that warrants such changes, the cost savings will be considerable.

Here are some general rules you can apply in high-speed automatic assembly.

- Ensure that parts can be easily separated from bulk and conveyed along the track of a vibratory or hopper feeder.
- Avoid parts that tangle; are flexible and fragile; have thin or tapered edges that can overlap; are sticky or oily.
- Use parts that are easily oriented, such as symmetrical parts or those with projections, notches, or other orienting features.

Because of the expert nature of the design requirements for automatic assembly, you will need to become knowledgeable in such design features or consult with experts in the field.

Consider Product Liability

Privity is a legal term meaning a direct relationship between two parties. When products of the past failed, causing harm, manufacturers argued that the product was distributed by a wholesaler or retailer and privity was absent. In one landmark case, *MacPherson vs. Buick Motor Company*, the plaintiff was driving a new car when one of its wheels fell off, resulting in injury. Buick declared that the defective axle came from another manufacturer, and therefore, it had no liability. The judge, however, ruled that Buick was liable because of its responsibility to remove danger from the car. The newness of the car eliminated negligence in maintenance of the owner. The product must not only be safe while in use, but also during distribution and retirement or discarding.

Potential product liability risk can be designed out of a product by following certain guidelines.

- Design to nationally recognized standards.
- Use components with statistical reliability.
- An accelerated life test can be valuable in discovering defects and disputing testimony of design defect in product liability suits.
- Make a worst-case analysis of the product.
- Drawings must have notes to manufacturing to eliminate hazards; for example, remove burrs or plating notes. A drawing without notes determining a quality standard can lose a liability suit.
- Record product development history and design decision reasoning.
- Consider shipping vibration, which can weaken parts not designed for abnormal fatigue.
- Use warning labels where appropriate.
- Include proper instructions for use.
- Use independent testing whenever possible.

Warranties

Warranties must also be considered when thinking about liability. There are three kinds of warranties: express, implied, and limited. Express warranties are defined by the Uniform Commercial Code (UCC) to be any promise made by the seller that influenced the sale and any description that influenced the sale; for example, pictures, ads, or brochures.

Implied warranties communicate that because the product is for sale, the manufacturer has made every effort to ensure the product is safe and certain minimum qualities exist.

In 1975, Congress passed the Magnuson-Moss Warranty Act in an attempt to clarify the extent of any warranty given by a manufacturer. This led to the limited warranty, which limits compensation to the buyer.

If you are in the development stages when design may be changed in light of possible faults, obviously the time and efforts are well worth it. The responsibility of the design lies with the inventor, as well as with the professional engineer.

Product Life Cycles

.ıere are four life cycle stages of a product.

- **Production.** This first cycle is the process of creating a usable product from raw material.
- **Distribution.** This second cycle occurs when the product is transferred to the consumer.
- **Consumption.** This third cycle is the use of the product by the customer.
- **Retirement.** This final cycle is the disposal of the product.

Each of these stages requires consideration during the design of a new product. The production of raw materials can present liabilities to the production or assembly worker and you must address these liability issues. Even distribution carries liability; if your product is improperly packaged and causes liability, you are responsible.

One such case involved a longshoreman who fell through a void in a large cardboard package. Even though the man was walking on the packaging, the courts felt the distributor should have been prepared for such events.

Maintain Certain Standards

Designing your product to established standards can be your best protection for reducing your product liability risk. Some important organizations you may wish to consider contacting for assistance are listed below.

American National Standards Institute – ANSI
11 West 42nd Street, 13th Floor
New York, NY 10036
(212) 642-4900

The ANSI is the main clearinghouse for standards.

American Society for Testing and Materials – ASTM
1916 Race Street
Philadelphia, PA 19103-1187
(215) 299-5400

The ASTM publishes more than 4,000 standards that identify test procedures and test equipment.

Consumer Product Safety Commission
5401 Westboard Avenue
Bethesda, MD 20207
(800) 638-2772 (Nationwide)

This agency protects the consumer from the manufacture and sale of hazardous products.

Environmental Protection Agency – EPA
401 M Street, SW
Washington, DC 20460
(202) 755-0707

The EPA protects the environment from many factors, including manufacturing operations.

Federal Information Center
(301) 722-9000
(800) 366-2998 (Nationwide)

This service provides pre-recorded messages and phone numbers for federal agencies.

Federal Trade Commission – FTC
Pennsylvania Avenue & 6th Street, NW
Washington, DC 20004
(202) 326-2222

The FTC warns the public when a product is unsafe.

Food and Drug Administration – FDA
5600 Fishers Lane
Rockville, MD 20857
(301) 443-6170

The FDA originated with the Food and Drug Act of 1906. Among many other products, cosmetics must conform to FDA standards.

National Fire Protection Assoc. – NFPA
P.O. Box 9101
Quincy, MA 02269-9101
(617) 770-3000
(800) 344-3555

The NFPA publishes all standards related to fire protection equipment. The *National Electrical Code* (NEC) is published under NFPA standards.

National Safety Council – NSC
1121 Spring Lake Drive
Itasca, IL 60143-3201
(708) 289-6061

The NSC devotes its efforts to accident prevention.

Occupational Safety and Health Administration – OSHA
1825 K Street, NW
Washington, DC 20006
(202) 634-7943

OSHA is responsible for conducting research for workplace safety.

Underwriters Laboratories – UL
333 Pfingsten Road
Northbrook, IL 60062
(708) 272-8800

UL is perhaps best known for the UL label, which is applied to products that pass rigorous testing, using one or more of its 350 standards. The UL label is well recognized as evidence of satisfactory design.

In addition, the second edition of *The Product Standards Index* by V. L. Roberts identifies many standard-writing organizations and lists standards that apply to various products. To obtain a copy, contact:

Pergamon Press/Elsevier Science, Inc.
Madison Square Station
P.O. Box 945
New York, NY 10160-0757
(212) 989-5800

Consider Form and Function

Much of what has been covered so far in this chapter falls within the realm of industrial design. Industrial designers are basically professional inventors who conceive ideas, build prototypes, research, and develop new products.

Industrial design came into being more than 60 years ago because of a public that demanded convenience in every aspect of their lives. They also demanded that convenience be attractive. New products had to not only look as though they were capable of doing their job, they also had to enhance the looks of the home or office. The industrial designer, therefore, had to be concerned with the form, color, and texture of a product, as well as its functionality.

These considerations are still very important today. Consumers many times still think of plastics as being inexpensive, glass as being breakable, aluminum or stainless steel as being long-lasting, steel as being strong, fine-grained wood as being expensive, and leather or silk as being elegant. Even texture and color affect a product's appeal. The mechanics of a product may require engineering and science, but designing the appearance is pure art.

Find Needed Materials and Assistance

In building your first prototype, you will most likely purchase your needed materials at a local hardware store or have it made at a local machine shop. Later, you will need to find industrial suppliers for larger quantities and also to avoid paying retail price. Part of the prototype process is finding future suppliers. Another benefit in dealing directly with the manufacturer is free samples. When was the last time a retail store offered you that?

The best source for obtaining needed materials and information is from a nearby manufacturer. To locate appropriate manufacturers, go to your city or county library's business and technology department and request a listing of its manufacturers' directories. Manufacturers' directories available at the library include:

- *MacRae's Blue Book*
- *Thomas Register*
- *U.S. Industrial Directory*

In particular, the *Thomas Register* is a good starting point. It consists of several volumes that list nearly everything under the sun, such as a company's address, phone number, product lines, and net sales per year. Additional sections include company catalogs and company profiles as well. Not only will the *Thomas Register* help you find materials, it will also help you find potential licensees and competitors. The *U.S. Industrial Directory* and *MacRae's Blue Book* also work well as additional research sources. All three sources should be used because some companies will only be listed in one of the three directories.

In addition to these directories, the public library also has numerous directories for specific regions and industries. Many libraries now have these catalogs and directories on computer databases for keyword searching. An additional listing of manufacturers' directories is featured in Chapter 4. Some other sources for finding prototype materials include:

Plasti-Glas
Building B
720 Sloan Avenue
Trenton, NJ 08619
(609) 587-1188
FAX (609) 587-3463

A good source of epoxy and urethane resins for model makers and prototypes.

Edmund Scientific Company
101 East Gloucester Pike
Barrington, NJ 08007-1380
(609) 573-6260
FAX (609) 573-6295

A source for science equipment and chemicals.

When building your prototype, you may need assistance in developing the materials required for your invention. Most manufacturing companies have employees whose job it is to solve the problems of potential or existing customers.

As a potential customer interested in doing business with a company, you have access to the company's engineers, designers, and salespeople. Their job is to assist you, even though a customer may use only a portion of the available services. The most effective way to obtain these and other services is to be sincere in dealing with a company and act professionally. You can reap benefits from using company experts; you may be their biggest customer someday.

Another method for obtaining prototype assistance is to check local schools, colleges, vocational and technical programs, and universities. Many of these schools require class projects and student assignments each year. This process of prototype building can produce a quality product that will be very inexpensive. On the downside, it may take several months to complete. Remember, you only have one year from completion of a working model of your invention to file a patent application.

One important point to keep in mind when using the services of others is that an unpaid prototype builder could become a legal partner in your invention. A good practice when having other people work on your invention is to have them sign a nondisclosure agreement and to get a receipt for your file for all paid work they do. An ounce of prevention initially can eliminate an unwanted partner later.

Tips for Building Your Own Prototype

Building your own prototype is probably one of the best aspects of inventing. You are the one uniquely qualified to develop your idea into a tangible product, and with a few tips, you may find that it is not as hard as you thought it would be.

One important aspect about building prototypes is attitude. Be creative, have fun, and try as many variations as possible with the invention. No professional could possibly share the excitement and enthusiasm you will feel when building your own prototype.

Don't let industrial processes intimidate you. The libraries are full of how-to books on most every process known. Injection molding was once done with hydraulic jacks and with plastic cooked in pots. Vacuum forming can be done at home using your stove, vacuum cleaner, and plaster of Paris. Molds for pouring lead, rubber, and plastic can be made out of auto-body putty. The tools to do almost anything are available, if you are willing to seek them out.

For example, you can make molds by using silicone adhesive. Simply form the silicone around a particular part you want to mold. This provides you with a mold for limited production. Since silicone can be bought at the hardware store for about $2 a tube, it can be a very inexpensive prototype tooling. Charcoal lighter fluid will thin most silicones, which can then be applied by brush. Going to the library and reading different formula books will give you other ideas as well.

One excellent book you may wish to read is *Ingenious Mechanisms For Designers and Inventors*. You can purchase a copy from the publisher.

Industrial Press, Inc.
200 Madison Avenue
New York, NY 10016
(212) 889-6330
FAX (212) 545-8327

Additional books for use in mechanical design are *507 Mechanical Movements* and *998 Curious Mechanical Movements*. Both books are available through their publisher.

Lindsay Publications, Inc.
P.O. Box 12
Bradley, IL 60915-0012
(815) 468-3668

Industry Processes

Often, inventors are not knowledgeable on all the processes that exist in industry. The list below will help familiarize you with some of the processes available.

Blow molding. A hollow extruded plastic tube is positioned so mold cavities close while air is forced into the tube, forcing plastic to take the shape of the mold. The blow-molding process is used in making, among other things, two-liter soda bottles.

Die casting. This process is inexpensive, fast, and accurate, but can only use nonferrous alloys because of their low melting temperatures.

Electric discharge machining (EDM). This is when machine operation employs direct electrical current to "arc" away metal.

Extrusion molding. This process entails the continuous formation of tubes, pipes, and shapes of metal, plastic, and other suitable materials through the use of forming dies.

High-pressure laminating. This process uses high heat and pressure to hold plastic to reinforcing materials that comprise the body of the finished product. It is used for formed shapes which need reinforcing.

Hobbing. A ductile metal billet is placed within a hardened retainer ring to be plunged into a formed cavity.

Injection molding. This is the process of extruding molten material into mold cavities, allowing the hot material to form and cool. This is normally used with plastic and powdered metals.

Investment casting. This is a metal-casting process. A wax model of the part is prepared and imbedded in a special slurry of refractory. After the slurry has been poured, it is vacuumed to remove air bubbles. When the refractory has set up and dried, it is placed in a high temperature oven and the material becomes fired, melting the wax and leaving a hollow void. Thereafter, molten metal is poured into the cavity remaining, sometimes by spin casting.

Lay-up. This process consists of a plastic manufacturing process that involves the use of an original pattern upon which a fiber cloth or mat-like fiberglass, burlap, or sisal is combined with catalyzed polyester or epoxy liquid resin to form a hardened shape.

Machining. By employing milling machines, either vertically or horizontally, it is possible to cut away metal, drill holes, or slot and shape, tap threads, and otherwise sculpt solid materials, such as metal, plastic, and wood.

Rotational molding. This is a process for making hollow parts using a prepolymerized liquid plastic resin.

Sand casting. This is a metal-forming process. A cavity is formed by pressing a pattern into a bed of sand. Molten metal is poured into the cavity and cools to harden. Generally, this process is used for rougher and sturdier parts, such as manhole covers, machinery bases, and structural framework.

Solvent molding. Based on the fact that when a mold is immersed in a solution and withdrawn, or when it is filled with a liquid plastic and then emptied, a layer of plastic film adheres to the sides of the mold. It is used for products like bathing caps.

Spin casting. A metal-casting process in which molten metal is centrifuged into the mold cavities, rather than poured in. Spin casting is used in making high-finish and accuracy parts.

Thermoforming/vacuum forming. A sheet of plastic is heated and drawn or pressured down over a pattern to create a finished shape. This is done to make covers and formed shapes. Plastics that can be thermoformed are acrylics, nylon, polyethylene, polystyrene or styrene, polyfluorocarbons, vinyls, polyvinylidene, acrylonitrile-butadiene-styrene (ABS), acetal resin, polypropylene and polycarbonates.

Transfer molding. This process is used for thermosetting plastics. The plastic is cured in a mold under heat and pressure, and it is usually used to facilitate the molding of intricate products with small, deep holes or numerous metal inserts.

21st Century Prototypes

For those of you who can afford to go all out on the prototype, there are two prototype processes that are relatively inexpensive to use for the small business. The first is stereolithography and the second is metal-spray moldmaking. The processes work well together.

Stereolithography, a process developed by 3D Systems, Inc. in Valencia, California, combines computer-aided design (CAD) with photocuring to build three-dimensional parts. The operation employs photocurable polymers that change from liquid to solid in the presence of ultraviolet light. A helium-cadmium scanning laser, similar to those in CD players, supplies the radiation. A stainless steel vat that contains the photopolymer, and a "slice" computer, make up the rest of the stereolithography apparatus (SLA).

First, CAD software converts the solid or surface data to a faceted triangle format. SLA software then "slices" the three-dimensional model into a series of two-dimensional cross sections, and defines each section's boundaries. It then fills the boundaries with structural cross hatching and constructs the top and bottom skins using a series of tightly spaced surface vectors. Controlled by computer-generated vector patterns, X-Y galvanometer mirrors direct the beam along the photopolymer's surface. As the mirrors translate, the beam cures and hardens the plastic. The operator, meanwhile, can watch each section's development on the slice computer's monitor. Although the process sounds like it still belongs in the future, the reality of the process shows just how one invention can assist in the building of another.

Once the stereolithography is complete, the metal-spray moldmaking process begins by spraying the plastic model with an atomized stream of molten metal. The metal, a Kirksite alloy developed by TAFA Inc., of Concord, New Hampshire, feeds into an arc spray gun as two electrically charged wires which intersect at the gun's head create a high-temperature arc. While the arc melts the feedstock, a 50 cubic foot per minute (cfm) jet of air blows the molten metal against the master. The particles interlock and solidify upon impact to form a dense, hard shell.

The molten particles of metal, because they are surrounded by the high-velocity air stream, do not damage the plastic master. The shell's temperature, in fact, never exceeds 150 degrees. Once removed from the master, the mold is placed in the cavity of a premachined aluminum block and backed up with an epoxy binder. The shell and block form the die at one-third the cost of the traditional tooling process. Lead time is also cut to about one-third. Although this method may not work for all applications, its success is growing fast and will soon spin off other improved methods.

Do-It-Yourself Shops

If you are a do-it-yourselfer, you need to locate an operation that provides a complete woodworking and machine shop for a monthly fee. These types of shops can often be found in the Yellow Pages under woodworking or hobby clubs. Do-it-yourself shops not only provide you with the resources to build your prototype, but they also expose you to many other skilled people who use the facilities. Most of these shops are inexpensive to join and offer expert help, a lucky find for any inventor.

Many inventors use these facilities to begin production before committing to production facilities. The "co-op" environment is also a plus for inventors seeking assistance. For instance, on visits to the local do-it-yourself shop, you could meet a member who is using new materials you have not seen or heard about before. To become more educated, from time to time, you could look over a few shoulders and most likely learn something new to use in your prototype.

The Inventor's Workshop

Your inventor's workshop can be important to the prototype of your invention. Your workshop may be the kitchen table, basement, or garage, or it may even be your whole house or apartment. Having a place to work and think is important because of the inspiration and attitude a special place can offer. Try putting an executive on a street corner to make that next big deal, and you will understand the importance of environment.

An ideal work space will have a drawing board for sketching or drawing plans, a library of resource materials, and of course, a work area for building that idea. Inventors' workshops are usually cluttered with scrap parts, hardware, and other odds and ends. Most inventors rarely throw anything away. Some workshops may include at least 20 years' worth of accumulated gadgets, broken appliances, and whatchamacallits, which are all treasured as a rare collection. Why go buy or build something when you already have something almost like it in the garage? To an inventor, that old toaster is just the part for that new neutron heater. Sometimes, just looking at your gadgets will help you create something new.

Mold-Making Materials for Your Workshop

Materials that inventors should keep around their workshops include the following:

Latex. This substance is easy to clean, water soluble, nontoxic, nonflammable, and good for up to 50 reproductions. Latex is very flexible and must be brushed on in thin layers. Latex is better for small to moderate-sized models of wood, ceramics, plaster, cement, water-based clay, synthetic and oil-based clay, brass, bronze, copper, glass, wax, and plastics. The best release agents are silicone spray, liquid wax, and polyvinyl alcohol. The best materials for casting in latex are urethane rubber, epoxy, polyester resins, fiberglass, plaster, cement, and concrete.

Plaster of Paris. Also known as casting plaster, it is inexpensive, readily available, has no odor, and is quick-setting. It is easy to mix and is also good for reinforcing flexible molds, such as latex. Plaster of Paris is good for both large and small molds and will last longer if you seal it with a lacquer or varnish. Good release agents for molds are polyvinyl alcohol, zinc stearate, or silicone spray. Materials suitable for using with plaster of Paris include polyester and epoxy resins, fiberglass, plaster, concrete, and urethane foam. When preparing a mold for fiberglass, seal the plaster of Paris with three or four coats of thinned shellac.

Rigid urethane. Also known as Trymer 9501 and rigid foam insulation, rigid urethane is an interesting material used for forming your own molds. It is easy to carve and shape and can be used to run vacuum-formed parts directly from a mold. The material is inexpensive and is used to make very large molds. Rigid urethane has been used to make parts as large as ten feet long and three feet high.

Room temperature vulcanizing rubber (RTV). RTV silicone and silicone sealer can be used up to 100 times for molds. It cures at room temperature; is nontoxic, flexible, durable; and has a good temperature resistance for casting wax and metals with low melting points. It needs 24 hours for curing and is good for small to medium-sized models. Models can be metal, ceramic, concrete, plaster, wood, wax, or glass. Release agents are not needed for most materials, although for works made from ceramics a petroleum jelly thinned with paint thinner works well. Materials best used for casting include candle wax, urethane foam, plaster, concrete, polyester resins, and metals with low melting points.

How to Find Prototype Builders

Although building your own prototype is recommended, there are times when it just can't be done. Finding professional help in this area can sometimes be difficult because such people are not always listed in the Yellow Pages under prototype builders. The best way to find a professional who could build your invention is to look for local manufacturers who work in related fields or look for industrial model builders.

The local library can also be a good source of prototype builders. Check out the state directories on business, as well as the *Thomas Register*. In addition, you may want to contact these two organizations, and obtain the directories they produce.

American Society for Testing and Materials – ASTM
1916 Race Street
Philadelphia, PA 19103
(215) 299-5400

This society of test labs publishes the *Directory of Testing Laboratories*.

American Council of Independent Laboratories – ACIL
1725 K Street, NW
Washington, DC 20006
(202) 877-5872

The ACIL can help you find a testing laboratory that will test your prototype for safety considerations. It also publishes a directory entitled, *Directory of the ACIL*, that lists its members.

For additional sources of information and assistance, see Appendix A.

Study Your Creation

Remember, the prototype phase of inventing is also an evaluation phase; an evolution takes place as your idea begins to take shape and gains that finished production look.

As your product develops throughout the prototype phase, take time to step back, evaluate, and study your creation. This is the most important stage in the product's development and a time to put your dreams to the test. If your invention can survive the prototype process, it will have a far better chance of surviving the manufacturing and marketing stages. The success of your invention starts when you turn your idea into something tangible.

6

Market Your Product

If opportunity doesn't knock, build a door. — Milton Berle

Learn the Market

Marketing your new idea or product is one of the most important stages in becoming successful. For those confident of their ability, knowledge, and determination, taking an invention to market will be a great adventure.

The reason so many inventors fail to get their ideas and concepts to the marketplace is their inability to adequately comprehend the importance of each step involved. If you are serious about turning your creativity into profits, you must master or at least understand marketing.

Maybe up to now you were interested in making a better product or advancing technology. Perhaps all you wanted to do was get rich quick, but none of that will happen until you attract customers. Understanding and targeting your customer is what marketing is all about. If your product satisfies a need or desire and the price is right, your job is much easier.

Marketing begins with a product idea (creativity), but successful marketing is complete when the product (your idea) is at the right place (distribution) at the right time (a little luck) at the right price (pricing), with effective communication to potential customers (sales promotion).

To have the right product at the right time, you must identify consumer needs or wants, preferences, and motivation. Become familiar with competitive products and activities, economic conditions, and government regulations. You must develop an intimacy with the market, understanding potential customers and how they think and act. Only then can you target your customer.

Think of your customer as buying an expectation of benefits. The buyer wants satisfaction from your product; your goal is to match that desire.

Preliminary Testing

One of the most common problems facing new products is inadequate testing in the marketplace. It isn't what the inventor or manufacturer thinks about the product that counts, but what the consumer thinks.

The best way to test your product is to expose it to the public. There is a simple do-it-yourself test that you can perform if you know or have access to at least 20 people, preferably as many as 50. These people should be objective and totally honest.

This test is really quite simple. All you have to do is to show them your product and ask some basic questions, such as:

- How much would they pay for the product?
- Would they buy it, if the price was comparable to that of the competition?
- What type of product are they using now, and why?

Now start a file and store the data you obtain from these people until the testing is completed. Once you have collected data from at least 20 people, go over the information and see exactly how many people would purchase your product. If only 1 out of 20 said yes, you have some serious problems, either with your marketing methods or with the product itself. Reevaluate your product.

Next, determine the power of your competitors by comparing notes on what product the people are currently using. Going up against a familiar product, without having a unique feature people want and need, could be considered marketing suicide. Using your data, determine roughly how much people would pay for your product. To do this, average out the prices you were given.

Now, if you really want to put your product to a good marketing test, calculate its profit potential. Take the average price as determined in your survey and subtract 25 percent for the retail markup — if it is a specialty item or is sold by hardware stores, subtract 40 percent — 10 percent for the cost of transporting the product to the store; 15 percent for advertising (if you intend to do any); 10 percent for warehousing; 5 percent for administration and your salary; and 5 percent for insurance.

Once all of these costs are subtracted from the average retail price, you will see what is left to produce the product. If the numbers look reasonably good, you have a product that has some profit potential. If the numbers are negative, you will have to work to correct this.

The table below is based on an item that, according to preliminary testing, should sell at retail for $10.

Cost Factors	**Amounts**	**Balance**
Retail price	$10.00	$10.00
Retail markup (–25%)	<2.50>	7.50
Transportation (–10%)	<1.00>	6.50
Advertising (–15%)	<1.50>	5.00
Warehousing (–10%)	<1.00>	4.00
Administration, salary (–5%)	<0.50>	3.50
Insurance (–5%)	<0.50>	3.00
Potential Profit		$ 3.00

If your product is a specialty widget item, the retail markup figure would be $4.00, and the potential profit would only be $1.50.

Now that you have displayed your product and received a preliminary response, it is time to try test marketing.

Test Marketing

Test marketing is the sampling of a limited quantity of products in the marketplace. The results of a marketing test will tell you about sales potential, projected production needs, and profits. The test will produce preliminary data for determining how and where to market. You will have complimented the product by critique and evaluation. In one sense, you are experimenting to see what happens when the product is exposed to the consumer.

What Does the Consumer Think?

One very important purpose of the market test is to find out what the consumer thinks. To do that, you must find your potential consumers, show them your product, and then listen to their responses. The results of your market test will be very important and should be taken seriously. The data should be used to make refinements in both your product and marketing efforts.

For example, one individual purchased a $10 license to become a street vendor to test his new product, and spent weekends on street corners testing his idea. He made about $800 a day selling the product out of his van. At the same time, he set up displays in local stores. In the stores, his product netted about $20 a week. He is now doing what his market test suggested and travels from town to town selling his product from his van. You never know where your market may be unless you experiment.

With test marketing, sometimes you have to show a little ambition and risk trying some selling yourself. Anyone can sit at a flea market on the weekend, form his or her own marketing study, and have some fun in the process.

For those who may not feel comfortable sitting on a street corner, a more conventional approach would be to display your product in local store space, a competitive environment where established distributors make their living. The challenge is to make them move over.

In order to receive precious shelf space in the appropriate store, you will need to speak with either the store owner or manager to learn the requirements. A professional approach to this is to leave the product in the car and personally approach the owner or manager. Introduce yourself, and ask to set up an appointment to talk about a new product — your product. At the appointment, listen and learn. A manager can provide a wealth of marketing information; ask him about providing space for a test-market display and what you would need to do to conform to his store's requirements. Most managers have the authority to purchase directly from you and are usually willing to give a new product a chance, if it is properly packaged.

If you are going to sell your product from a store shelf or even a street corner, remember to use your imagination for unconventional and refreshing marketing angles. Continue to explore the data to determine what other directions you also may take.

Pricing

Some products are so similar and competition so well entrenched that industry pricing practices must be followed closely. Competition sets the price, and you, as a newcomer to the market, will generally want to sell at or below the competition's prices.

The strategy of making a better product and selling it for less than the competition is a good strategy only if the better product costs less to make than the competitor's product. There are three points to consider in pricing your product: demand, cost, and profit.

Demand Factor

Demand orientation means prices are set by market forces. The inventor can influence demand through such things as product differences, services, and quality compared to competitive or substitute products. Different product features and benefits can be offered to different market segments. Even with demand orientation, the consumer must perceive the value of the product to be higher than the price to be paid for it.

Cost Factor

Cost-oriented pricing is based upon considerations within the company, including the markup above the cost to produce. Markup pricing is most widely used because of its simplicity and ease of understanding. Markup pricing does not generally consider cost variations and the influence of demand for the product.

Markup pricing is generally used as a price limit, or a minimum price at which sales will be profitable. Many times, a new market will start initial pricing by demand factors, sometimes referred to as "what the market will bear," later moving to markup pricing.

Profit Factor

Profit-oriented pricing is based on price versus volume versus profit. Often, a break-even analysis is used to consider fixed cost, variable cost, sales volume, and resulting profits from sales in order to skim as much profit off the top as possible. Profit-oriented pricing is also known as skimming the market; this is when a product is introduced at a high price to take advantage of the high profits available from customers willing to pay to be the first to own the product. After the cream of the market is taken, you then reduce the price to attract the mass market to the product and to meet new competition. The high profits obtained during the skimming phase will, of course, invite many competitors into the market.

One of the best examples of this type of marketing is the calculator business of the 1970s. The first pocket calculators cost around $69.95, and today, that same type of calculator sells for about $1.00.

For additional information on pricing, examine *Pricing Practices and Strategies,* published by The Conference Board.

The Conference Board, Inc.
845 Third Avenue
New York, NY 10022
(800) 872-6273

Marketing Strategies

Once your product is available to the public, enhance your chances of success through publicity. Publicity doesn't always mean prime time exposure or a television commercial. Actually, the best publicity for test marketing a product can come at no charge. There are arrays of media sources out there just waiting to cover a story of local interest. You just need to know how to approach them.

News Releases

News releases are one of the best ways to approach media sources — such as local newspapers, magazines, and radio and television stations — for getting publicity. A news release needs to answer the who, what, where, when, why, and how of any product or event and should be clearly written and concise. Direct the release to a specific individual at the media source, such as the news editor or business reporter, and be sure to always include a contact name and phone number on the first page of a news release in case the editor or reporter wants to follow up.

Writing a news release on your own is not a difficult task, but it does take some practice and it follows several general rules. If you are inexperienced in writing news releases, consider getting advice from a public relations professional or reading a book or article on the topic. Some basic items you should know before contacting a media source for possible publicity include:

- Know what segment of the population you are trying to reach through the release, for example, your customer or media contact.
- Recognize newsworthy items and story ideas, such as a new product.
- Get the media's attention with good contacts.
- Format and write a news release properly.

Local Newspapers

After you prepare a news release, you can send it to the local newspaper. After a few days, follow up with the reporter or editor to see if he received the release and if a possible story could occur. Normally, newspapers will not pass up a story of local interest. Newspapers offer a great avenue to tell the world about what you are doing.

Magazines

Magazines are another valuable source of publicity for new products and business news, and you should research which magazines would be most interested in your news releases.

To determine your best possibilities for a suitable magazine, go to the library and review the *Standard Rate and Data Service Book*, which lists some 12,000 publications, including all the magazines within your particular market or industry. No matter what your invention's category, there is probably a publication that covers it. Other good sources to review while at the library include:

- *The Standard Periodical Directory*
- *Ulrich's International Periodicals Directory*
- *Writer's Resource Guide*

Once you compile a list of appropriate magazines, contact each one and request a media kit. A media kit will contain the magazine's advertising rates, demographics, and editorial features and department. From this information, you can better decide which magazines to target.

To properly approach these magazines, use a news release kit consisting of a cover letter explaining that you would like to be listed in the magazine's new product section, a description of the new product, including features and benefits, and a sharp 5 X 7-inch black-and-white photo. Always send your kit to the attention of the editorial department and indicate on the envelope that dated material is enclosed.

One last point to mention here is that some magazines may require several months lead time, and some magazines now charge to list your product within their new product sections. You must determine if the price for that publicity is reasonable for the coverage you may obtain.

Radio and Television

In addition to contacting local newspapers and magazines, you can also send news releases to local radio and television stations. Often, news departments will do a story on local business and product development. In addition, you can contact a station's sales department to see about purchasing time to advertise.

Many cable television stations will broadcast commercials for your product on a percentage basis, which includes production costs. Normally, products of interest to these stations are the higher-profit items, which sell for less than $24. For air time and production of the commercial, expect to give away at least 50 percent of the profit.

Talk to local radio stations about using public service announcements (PSAs), or local community spots. Use every possibility to expose your product and yourself; don't be shy. The publicity you create for yourself and your product will reach thousands of prospective customers, which in turn, will mean greater profits. For example, Lee Mauck, who invented the Res-Q-Ring, an innovative ring buoy, discovered the importance of publicity when he found that Oklahomans, not having an ocean nearby, had little interest in his invention. So Lee devised a publicity stunt by renting a helicopter and jumping into the Arkansas River to be rescued by his new invention. He, of course, called the local television stations ahead of time and invited them to watch.

The publicity stunt worked so well that the local stations put the story on The Associated Press, where it was picked up by other stations across the country. Not only was the story seen nationwide, but Lee was invited to demonstrate his invention on the network television show, *That's Incredible*. The prime-time exposure Lee received would have cost him hundreds of thousands of dollars had he paid for the air time. Instead, his product was launched to its ultimate success when investors called from around the country wishing to invest in the product. Most importantly, Lee believed in his invention enough to put his life on the line — he is a serious inventor who deserves his success. A list of companies that publish guides and directories of television contacts, shows, and stations include:

Bacon's, Inc.
332 South Michigan Avenue
Chicago, IL 60604

Publishers of *Bacon's Radio/TV Directory.*

Broadcast Publications, Inc.
1735 DeSales Street, NW
Washington, DC 20036

Publishers of *Broadcast Magazine.*

Larimi Communication
5 West 37th Street
New York, NY 10018

Publishers of *TV News.*

Public Relations Publishing Company
888 Seventh Avenue
New York, NY 10106

Publishers of *The Professional's Guide to Public Relations Services.*

Television Digest, Inc.
1836 Jefferson Plaza, NW
Washington, DC 20036

Publishers of *Television & Cable Factbook.*

Trade Shows

Trade shows are another effective way to market your product, and even though this type of marketing costs money up front, trade shows put thousands of potential customers in one place, willing and seeking to buy new products. Many beginning companies use trade show successes to finance their start-up costs, as well as to support their marketing studies.

There are more than 8,000 trade shows each year in the United States alone, catering to every industry from automobiles to toys. Many success stories come from trade shows. For example, there were two women who spent $500 on a booth to promote slip-free socks at a children's-wear show and made $10,000 in one day, and there is the owner of Contemporary Designs, who wrote more than $14,000 in orders in just one day at a boutique show in New York City.

Many trade shows now assign booth locations by the lottery method. You may find your booth at the front door or next to your biggest competitor with its high-tech, expensive booth which makes your booth look inferior. Before you attend a trade show, visit a professional display maker, if not to purchase, at least to look at a professionally made booth. Projecting a company image is very important at trade shows, and the impression you leave will stay with potential customers. An important marketing tip to mention here is to have some kind of advertising giveaway or gimmick. Small samples are always very effective whenever possible, but even if it is a promotional key chain, use the opportunity to develop return customers. In Appendix C — located at the back of this book — you will find a partial listing of trade shows and the approximate months in which they occur. For a more comprehensive list of U.S. trade shows, refer to the following directories at your local library.

- *Annual Directory of Trade and Industrial Shows*
- *Directory of North American Fairs, Festivals and Expositions*

In addition, Appendix C features listings for international inventors' conventions and European trade fairs. For further updated information on European trade fairs, there are several publications available from the U.S. Department of Commerce, including:

- *Europe Now;*
- *European Trade Fairs: A Guide for Exporters;* and
- *German Trade Fairs: A Handbook for American Exhibitors and Exporters.*

To request these publications, write to:

Publication Distribution
U.S. Department of Commerce
Room H1617M
Washington, DC 20230

In addition, The Oasis Press/PSI Research publishes a comprehensive guide to exporting titled *Export Now: A Guide for Small Businesses.*

The Oasis Press/PSI Research
300 North Valley Drive
Grants Pass, OR 97526
(541) 479-9464
(800) 228-2275 (Nationwide)

Marketing Cons

In getting your product to the market, you may be enticed by a number of companies promoting themselves as invention brokers or marketing experts. And marketing experts they are, collectively making as much as $100 million a year. Unfortunately, this money is made preying on people who need marketing and development assistance.

These companies usually advertise in tabloids, on the radio, late-night television programs, and in magazines. The names change so often that there is no use in listing them. Many people have tried to stop these companies, but as long as there are people willing to pay, they are here to stay, providing phony marketing services, which can cost up to $20,000.

Warning Signs for Spotting Marketing Scams

There are several telltale approaches that usually accompany a marketing scam, such as:

- Free evaluations;
- Recommending further development while at the same time praising the product;
- Refusal to work on commission;
- Refusal to disclose other clients; and
- Refusal to discuss the company or its background.

Often, con artists will imply that the U.S. Patent and Trademark Office's disclosure document program offers patent protection. Once you have spotted a marketing company con, your best course of action is to simply stay away and warn others.

One such con artist laid his trap in Tulsa, Oklahoma. He tricked 32 inventors into paying him cash. By the time warrants were issued for his arrest, he was long gone. It is unfortunate that some very creative people paid someone to do what they could have done themselves and wound up losing their life savings. So be cautious and beware.

Package Your Product to Sell

The last time you were in a store, did you notice the hundreds of products along the aisles? On any crowded shelf, did a particular product grab your attention? If so, you were most likely attracted by the packaging.

Often, products are actually hidden away, tightly sealed within the confines of a box or package. If the packaging does not promote an immediate interest in the product, it is contributing to the failure of that product. Packaging can spell either success or failure for your product. Think what your response would be if you saw roses packaged in tin cans or a coat sold in a sealed box.

The first impression a prospective customer gets of your product is its packaging. Visually, you must ensure quality and confidence in the product. Appropriate packaging will effectively display your product in its best light to a targeted market.

Since packaging contributes so much to your product's chance for success, you should consider professional assistance in designing your package. Packaging designers and industrial designers can be located in the Yellow Pages and can contribute significantly to the market appeal of your product. If you are not in a position to hire an expert in packaging, you will find it beneficial to visit the library for information on marketing trends and studies, which are usually located in the research and technical sections.

Your package must present a clean, efficient, and attractive way of getting a product from the manufacturer to the consumer. There are many kinds of packaging to choose from, and the product itself usually has a way of determining the outcome. Today's packages must not only be attractive, they must also be easy to load, resistant to damage, simple to pack and unpack for bulk shipment, and lightweight.

Packaging is important enough to be one of the largest categories of patents, and if you are doing a patent search, check class 229 for some unique packaging ideas. If you are still not convinced of the importance of packaging, consider that Procter & Gamble invested millions of dollars in packaging Pringles® potato chips, a product which had more advertising about the package than the product itself. The quality or novelty of packaging is an important factor in marketing consumer goods.

Another consideration is to make your packaging serve more than one purpose. Can your package be used as the display in the store? Will it deter shoplifters? Can it sit on a shelf as well as hang on a peg? Your packaged product should sell itself. Be innovative and enthusiastic about this area and gain a better chance for success. A good resource on package design is the book, *The Silent Salesman: How to Develop Packaging that Sells*. Check your local library or bookstore.

Create a Professional Approach

In the same way you package a product to sell, you must also package yourself to sell. Professionals like dealing with other professionals. Being businesslike will increase your chances of success tenfold over being a nonprofessional. Consider an inventor who complained he never received a reply from his letters to manufacturers. Come to find out he was handwriting his letters on notebook paper. Furthermore, the letters were not sent to the attention of a specific person, and his letters were most likely being trashed by the first secretary who opened them. Quite simply, his letters gained little or no respect in the business world.

After learning that businesspeople rarely consider inventors to have good sales potential, he resubmitted the letter. Instead of handwriting the letter, he typed out a request for a quote from a particular person. He used his business letterhead, and he even had the letter meter-stamped at the post office to give it that professional look. This inventor not only received a prompt reply, but also a company catalog, sale ads, and free samples, all of which resulted from creating a professional appearance. If you expect to be treated professionally, you must act professionally.

Create a Quality Letterhead

If you wish to come up with some inexpensive letterhead to use for your correspondence, go to the local art store or business supply store and purchase some rub-on letters, also known as dry transfer lettering. A sheet will usually cost about $5. Pick a professional-looking style you like and apply your company name, address, and telephone number on a clean 8 1/2" X 11" sheet of paper. It may take a couple of tries to master the art of using rub-on letters, but generally it is pretty easy. Creating your own letterhead is only another avenue for using your creative talent and adding to your professional approach. If you own a personal computer or have access to one, you can design your own letterhead, using any one of several graphics software programs. Once you have your personal letterhead, go to a local printer or copy shop and run off some copies on good quality paper and store the original for future use.

Follow Professional Phone Tips

In addition to appearing professional on paper, you will also want to create a professional image over the phone. Many inventors are not used to dealing with large companies — this can be apparent when they try to reach someone by telephone. When the person you need is not available, leave a message and number where you can be reached. Constantly calling until you reach someone is unprofessional. It is always a good idea to keep notes of every phone conversation. Write down the who, when, and where of your conversations; an inventor's logbook is the best place to keep this information. Treat all phone contacts as though they are very important. In general, remember to act professionally and businesslike with every opportunity, and always think success.

Choose a Company Name

If you don't have a company name, get one. Doing business under a company name costs little or nothing. You do not have to incorporate a company to use a business name. While some states require that you register a company name, the cost is usually minimal. Check with your secretary of state's office and county clerk for any required business name filings and fees. When choosing a name for your business, consider the importance of the name. A name like "Barney and Charlie's Inventions" may not sound professional, while using the initials and calling the business the BCI Company would certainly sound more professional and garner more respect.

Consider Trademarks, Logos, and Brand Names

An important factor in successful packaging is the proper use and design of your company identity. For example, think about such names as the First Security National Bank, Great Northern Railroad, or Transcontinental Airlines. These names reflect a powerful and imposing nature, in the same way names like Bud's Hot Dog Stand, Whiz Bang Plumbers, or Frank's Bar and Grill imply a totally different feel, even though they may be appropriate for what they do. When you mix them up a little and get names like The First National Hot Dog Stand, Frank's Bank, and Whiz Bang Airlines, you see how a name can imply a feeling about the product and even the company behind the product.

Your company name should be appropriate to your product line, easy to read and, most importantly, easy to remember. An easily identifiable and attractive logo, brand name, or company name will add substantially to repeat sales and integrity, and will promote familiarity, confidence, and appeal in the product.

When your logo or brand name is created, it is a good idea to file for a trademark, which is covered in Chapter 3. A trademark will give immediate protection for your logo or brand name and can be important for future licensing possibilities. Many states charge only $25 to $50 for state trademark protection, and you may obtain the needed form by calling your secretary of state's office. Seek professional assistance when designing your logo. If you do not have that option, go to the library or bookstore to study such topics as color selection for marketing appeal, design symmetry, style selection, and current marketing trends. Other study aids include clip-art books and printers' paste-up books. It can also be very enlightening to look at different logos and packaging layouts used for goods already on store shelves. Remember, most of these packages have cost the companies using them thousands of dollars to develop and test. Other sources for ideas on trademarks, logos, and company and brand names include:

- *The Company Image: Building Your Identity and Influence in the Marketplace.*

  Wiley Press
  605 Third Avenue
  New York, NY 10158-0012
  (212) 850-6000
  (800) 225-5945

- *Entrepreneurs: The Men and Women Behind Famous Brand Names and How They Made It.*

  G.K. Hall
  866 Third Avenue
  New York, NY 10022
  (212) 702-6789
  (800) 257-5755

- *The Name Game: How to Name a Company or Product.*

  Dow Jones & Company, Inc.
  200 Liberty Street
  New York, NY 10281
  (212) 416-2000

- *Naming Your Business and Its Products and Services.*

  The P. Gaines Publishing Company
  P.O. Box 2253
  Oak Park, IL 60303
  (708) 524-9033

Long-Term Marketing

Consider that 50 percent of the consumer products now on the shelves were not there five years ago. The average lifespan of a consumer product is only about five years, and if you do not improve your product, someone else will. Of the products currently available for consumer use, only 25 percent will survive more than five years.

One fact that inventors do not consider in the beginning is that when marketing slows down, so do profits. When starting out, consider the long-range plans that must accompany the excitement of seeing your product on the shelf. Remember, profits, and only profits, keep distributors, store owners, and manufacturers happy.

When marketing your product, be thinking of new ideas for improvements and derivative products. If you have already established a place in the market, use it to explore new products which may have the same potential. You may even be able to help another inventor get to the market. Remember, marketing is finding out what people want and giving it to them.

One effective way of predicting future marketing trends is to read as many trade publications as possible. A company's success on the market may even be enhanced by updating its packaging to reflect new trends.

For example, one company that makes elaborate fishing-lure carrying cases began exploring the market more thoroughly. As a result, the company changed its focus to the medical industry after discovering that paramedics were in need of specialized carrying cases similar to the one the company was already making for the fishing industry. The medical industry was also an easier market to target. Always remain flexible and listen to market demand. Your survival depends upon it.

Terms and Standards Used in Industry

An important part of marketing is offering a quality product. Many times, inventors find their own manufacturing resources limited and they must use outside sources to produce their product in larger quantities. When this happens, they have to depend upon others to supply quality products. In order to assure this, they need to speak the same language. The following is a discussion of the more commonly used terms in industry.

Standard Industry Classification

To maintain some uniformity of data, states, counties, cities, and the private-sector, directories and publications have adopted the U.S. method of identifying industry by using Standard Industry Classification (SIC) numbers. These numbers identify companies by industry category and range from two-digit to eight-digit numbers.

The two-digit numbers are used to designate basic industries such as mining, chemicals, and agriculture. As the number of digits increases, so does the detail of identification. The eight-digit number and the Not Elsewhere Classified (NEC) sections specifically list product categories.

Many local government and private-sector directories will vary the number of identifying digits. For example, a company might have one or more SIC numbers. You can use SIC numbers to identify similar industries and similar companies. The U.S. Department of Commerce and the Bureau of the Census publish handbooks explaining the SIC numbers and how to use them. You can usually find them at the library.

Pantone Matching System

One industry standard you will use in any color selection will be the Pantone Matching System (PMS) standard. PMS serves as an international color standard for selecting color.

For example, if you called for Pantone 3395 C as a product color, the manufacturer would know you wanted a green, which was seven and one-half parts Pantone Green, one-half part Pantone Yellow and eight parts Pantone Transparent White; or, in percentages, 46.9 percent green, 3.1 percent yellow, and 50 percent transparent white. This procedure leaves no room for error and your product will be exactly the color you selected. *Pantone Color Formula Guides* are available at most art supply stores.

Other Standards

If you have a product that is flexible in any way, and if you wish to detail the exact hardness of the material, you would use either the Rockwell or Brinnell standards, or the Durometer for flexible materials. For machine threads of screws and bolts you would rely on Society of Automotive Engineers (SAE) and International Standards Organization (ISO) standards. If your product is used by the government or military, you will probably have to build to Military Specifications (MIL). When indicating a surface finish, you should use American Standard Surface Texture (ASST) standards.

The reason for having such precise measurements in industry is simple. If two pieces must fit precisely, the possibility of a misfit is 50/50. If ten parts must fit precisely, the possibility for error increases considerably. This is known as the "fault tree" in design engineering.

Selling to Department Stores

To deal directly with the larger department stores, you must have a comprehensive business plan. The department store buyer will want to know who is going to manufacture your product, who your vendor is, and in what quantities you are going to make the product. Do you have a cost analysis available that details how much it takes to make the product, what the profits to the representative are, and how much your profit is? In general, you must be able to show, from beginning to end, each stage of the product. See Chapter 7 for information on preparing a business plan.

You will find many department stores usually deal only with manufacturers or agents on their approved list. If you do not have proper representation or a manufacturer ready to produce your product, it will take longer to get in to see someone, if you get in at all. If a department store accepts your product, you must be able to supply it with sizeable quantities in a short period of time.

Many new products fall in the housewares category, so if you do not have a vendor, but one is required, you can obtain a list of manufacturers and vendors in your area by writing to:

National Housewares Manufacturers Assoc.
1324 Merchandise Mart
Chicago, IL 60654

Distribution

The methods used in moving your product from production to consumption are key external sources that can affect your pricing, sales volume, and success. There are three main types of distribution.

- Direct marketing. The manufacturer sells directly to the consumer through its own sales force.
- One-level distribution. Typically a retailer, sales agent, or manufacturer sells directly to a retail outlet.
- Two-level distribution. The product moves through a wholesaler and then a retailer, or in industrial marketing, a sales agent and a wholesaler or distributor.

You may be wondering why a manufacturer would use so many middlemen, risking a loss of profits and control. Middlemen are used because of their efficiency and the increased distribution they give a product. Because of their experience, specialization, contacts, and scale of operation, they can distribute your product for less money than you could yourself. To create good distribution, you need to:

- Research information for planning and facilitating exchange.
- Promote the product (distributors often provide this service).
- Contact prospective buyers.
- Match your product to a buyer's requirements, such as grading, assembling, packaging, financing, and the like.
- Negotiate the price and terms.
- Distribute, which is the transportation and storage of the product.
- Finance the distribution, which can sometimes be included by the distributor serving as an agent for collecting and dispersal of funds.
- Take a risk because the product is out of your hands and has yet to be sold.

In evaluating which type of distribution is best for you, consider that when the number of customers is large and geographically dispersed, and when customers tend to buy in small quantities on a frequent basis, you should use long channels of distribution with many middlemen at each level. Products that are bulky in relation to their value require channels that minimize the shipping distance and number of middlemen handling the product. Usually the best reason for using middlemen is to transfer some very specific tasks, including:

- Transit of goods;
- Advertisement to inform and influence buyers;
- Storage of inventory from which orders are filled; and
- The ability to search out and communicate with buyers.

Selecting a middleman is an extremely important function and should be done carefully. To evaluate a distributor's potential, look at the person's years in business, growth record, cooperativeness, and overall reputation.

Communicate with the Consumer

Marketing is communication, and in order to communicate with your prospective customer, you must consider one or more communication methods. Besides public relations or publicity that was discussed earlier under marketing strategies, your other options include using advertising, product sales literature, and personal selling.

Advertising

Advertising is a paid form of impersonal presentation and promotion and is used to create awareness of a product, in particular its features and benefits. Advertising motivates the consumer to see, buy, use, or gain additional information about the product. Too much glitz, and the product gets lost. Even if your product has a dozen features, present only the best two or three. Later, you can display all your features on the packaging, but a long list of features in an ad or a commercial will lose the reader's attention quickly.

Product Sales Literature

Product sales literature should be both factual and dramatic and contain all the information necessary to help the prospective customer make a decision to purchase. Good sales literature will include highlights of features, performance data, specifications, photographs, and illustrations that will help the consumer evaluate your product. Don't forget to include ordering information, a company address, telephone numbers, and where the product can be purchased.

Personal Selling

Personal selling consists of discussions with and presentations to consumers in person or by phone. Effective personal selling usually consists of informing the customers and helping them buy. It should be honest and straightforward. No matter how you approach consumers, if they have a real need for the product, and you have the right price, at the right place, at the right time, they will buy.

Helpful Marketing Resources

For increasing your chances of success, it can't be emphasized enough how important it is for you to understand your market and acquire all the knowledge you can about it.

The best and most inexpensive way to gain an edge in marketing is through reading as much material as possible on the subject. Reading a book is never a waste of time. You always learn something new; it is how you use the information that is important.

Marketing Books

Marketing your products can seem overwhelming at first, but with the right information and research, you should be able to begin developing your own marketing strategies. Some of the marketing books listed below may prove especially helpful.

- *The Complete Book of Product Publicity Guide* is a comprehensive coursebook that offers ways to increase sales.

  American Management Assoc. – AMA
  135 West 50th Street
  New York, NY 10020
  (518) 891-5510

- *Know Your Market: How to Do Low-Cost Market Research* provides information you can use to conduct your own research with practical marketing tools and techniques.

  The Oasis Press/PSI Research
  300 North Valley Drive
  Grants Pass, OR 97526
  (541) 479-9464
  FAX (541) 476-1479
  (800) 228-2275 (Nationwide)

- *Marketing Without Advertising* provides information on low-cost marketing options.

  Nolo Press
  950 Parker Street
  Berkeley, CA 94710-9867
  (510) 549-1976
  (800) 992-6656 (Nationwide)

- *National Trade and Professional Association Directory* is very helpful in locating industry sources for doing market research and developing mailing lists. It is available at most libraries.
- *Power Marketing for Small Business* is a hands-on, easy-to-read book that details all aspects of marketing for the beginner.

  The Oasis Press/PSI Research
  300 North Valley Drive
  Grants Pass, OR 97526
  (541) 479-9464
  FAX (541) 476-1479
  (800) 228-2275 (Nationwide)

- *Rand McNally Commercial Atlas and Marketing Guide* is a great resource for finding out about regional buying incomes, retail sales information, and population centers. It is available at most libraries and bookstores.

Selling to the Government

If you are interested in exploring selling your product to the federal government, write to:

General Services Administration
Federal Supply Service
1734 New York Avenue, NW
Washington, DC 20406

Mailing Lists

Mailing lists can be very useful in marketing your new product, but only if they are well-researched and up-to-date. In your research, you will learn your target market, so be sure your mailing lists contain only those contacts or prospects that reflect your target customer. Here are some resources that will help you get started on compiling mailing lists.

America Business Information
5711 South 86th Circle
P.O. Box 27347
Omaha, Nebraska 68127
(402) 593-4500
FAX (402) 331-1505

American Business Lists
5711 South 86th Circle
Omaha, NE 68127
(402) 592-9000
FAX (402) 331-1505

Standard Rate & Data Service
3004 Glenview Road
Wilmette, IL 60091-9970
(708) 256-6067
FAX (708) 375-5001

Magazines

Marketing magazines provide information and a potential media source for publicizing your product. Two you may be interested in are:

- *Advertising Age* has a feature entitled *Idea Marketplace*, and provides an in-depth look at the advertising world.
- *Sales and Marketing Management* features an annual *Survey of Buying Power* that contains comprehensive data on population, retail sales, and buying incomes.

Direct Mail Marketing Books

Since you can easily control mailing quantities when using direct mail, it can be an economical medium for your overall marketing strategy. You can create unique promotional pieces to emphasize your product's features and benefits. Consult the direct mail publications below to learn more about this marketing communication strategy.

- *A Business Guide to the Federal Trade Commission's Mail Order Rule.*

  Federal Trade Commission – FTC
  Pennsylvania Avenue & 6th Street, NW
  Washington, DC 20580
  (202) 326-2222

- *The Directory of Mail Order Catalogs.*

  Grey House Publishing, Inc.
  Pocket Knife Square
  Lakeville, CT 06039
  (203) 435-0868

- *Mail Order Legal Guide.*

  The Oasis Press/PSI Research
  300 North Valley Drive
  Grants Pass, OR 97526
  (541) 479-9464
  (800) 228-2275 (Nationwide)

- *Mail Order Success Secrets.*

  St. Martin's Press
  175 Fifth Avenue
  New York, NY 10010
  (212) 674-5151

Toy Research

If your creative business idea involves toys, a valuable source of market research information would be:

Excel Development, Inc.
7007 Dakota Avenue
Chanhassen, MN 55317
(612) 934-1200
FAX (612) 934-1118

Government Publications

Contact these agencies to request their lists of marketing publications.

Customer Services
Data User Services Division
U.S. Bureau of the Census
Washington, DC 20233

For demographic and economic statistics for marketing purposes, send one dollar for a sample *Factfinder for the Nation*, the newsletter published by the U.S. Department of Commerce/U.S. Bureau of the Census.

Superintendent of Documents
U.S. Government Printing Office
Washington, DC 20402
(202) 512-1800

Call for a listing of publications available through this office.

U.S. Small Business Administration – SBA
P.O. Box 30
Denver, CO 80201-0030
(800) 368-5855

Call for a listing of SBA publications.

Women-in-Business Organizations

Donald Trump move over. The new entrepreneur of the 90s is more likely to be named Donna. The past may have taught us that men were more likely to be the movers and shakers of the business world, but that is all changing now. Women are quickly becoming the most common and the most successful entrepreneurs in the United States. According to the U.S. Small Business Administration (SBA), over the last 15 years the number of women-owned businesses has almost doubled. More than one-third of all businesses are now owned by women. Women are becoming more knowledgeable about their opportunities and are taking full advantage of these changes in the global market of the 90s. On average, 75 percent of all new businesses started by women succeed, compared to only 25 percent of those started by men.

Federal and state governments have increased their special programs and information sources to help women businessowners. Even with women-owned businesses prospering better than men-owned businesses, government agencies still consider women-owned businesses "disadvantaged" and give them preferences when bidding on government contracts. For example, women-owned businesses were awarded more than $2 billion in federal prime contracts last year, compared to only $180 million almost ten years ago. That is an increase of more than tenfold. The SBA sees women as an emerging and powerful group of businessowners over the next couple of decades. As a result, the SBA has put women's business ownership specialists at more than 100 SBA offices all over the country. Some of the resources available for women in business include:

Congressional Caucus for Women's Issues
2471 Rayburn Building
Washington, DC 20515
(202) 225-6740

This group keeps track of women's issues across the country and helps introduce new legislation to help women-owned businesses.

Office of Women's Business Ownership
U.S. Small Business Administration
409 3rd Street, SW
Washington, DC 20416
(202) 205-6673

Through the Women's Network for Entrepreneurial Training (WNET), you can be paired up with a successful mentor. In addition, this office provides seminars on the government procurement process.

Women's Bureau
Office of the Secretary
U.S. Department of Labor
200 Constitution Avenue, NW
Washington, DC 20210
(202) 219-6652

This bureau provides free publications on women's business issues.

National Association of Women Business Owners
1100 Wayne Avenue, Suite 830
Silver Spring, MD 20910
(301) 608-2590
FAX (301) 608-2596

This organization provides education and training to its members. It also promotes business ownership by women and serves as a forum through which women can establish themselves in the business world.

7

Where to Find Financing

Obstacles are things a person sees when he takes his eyes off his goal. — E. Joseph Cossman

The Business Plan

It has been said that a person without a plan is a person planning to fail. A business plan is your blueprint for success. A business plan is an objective, written review of your business concept that identifies areas of weaknesses and strengths, pinpoints needs, and helps you plan and achieve your business goals. It gives you a clear idea of the obstacles that lie ahead and ways to get around them. There are a dozen reasons why you need a business plan, but most business plans are written for bankers, investors, or accountants and are used as a basis for a business to obtain start-up funding. To succeed in bringing your idea to the marketplace, you will need financing to ensure a strong start up and a continuous, sound financial backing. Even if you never intend to talk to a venture capitalist or bank, and even if you don't intend to make a lot of money, you still need a solid business plan to guide you.

Plan Your Success

A sound business plan requires an investment in both time and resources. Yet, it is not just an array of information: it is a guide that has been thoroughly researched. A business plan is your map to indicate where you are going and how you are going to get there. Before starting your business plan, you will need to clarify some points that you may have only vaguely considered up to now.

Consider these questions.

- What exactly is your product?
- How much do you intend to spend on advertising?
- What are your goals?
- How will you approach your market?
- Have you given your product a fair evaluation?
- Who is helping you in your business?
- Do you really understand your market?
- How big and where is your market?
- What are you willing to do to stay in business?
- Are you burning bridges behind you?

How to Prepare a Business Plan

There is no single format you must follow when it comes to researching and writing a business plan. But there is a format that is typical of most successful plans, and you can add to or delete from that format as required. Every business plan should contain an executive summary, a business history, a product analysis, a market analysis, an analysis of the competition, a manufacturing report, an operation management analysis, and some financial projections.

The guidelines below will assist you in answering important questions and laying out your business plan. Even if a topic does not seem to fit your present needs, you should consider including it for future reference when your company begins to expand.

General Introduction

To begin, write a paragraph or two as if you were explaining what your business does to a total stranger. Include the unique features of your product or company. Also include a projection of the future of your business and a report on where your customers are now and where they will be in the future.

The Executive Summary

This section of your plan should be a serious sales pitch; it is where you describe the need for your product and business. The executive summary should be a two- to five-page overview designed to draw attention to your product or company. If you are using the business plan to obtain financing, the executive summary will be the first thing a venture capitalist will read.

The executive summary should include a description of your product and business, target market, advantages over the competition, and who is running the business. Emphasize any special skill and experience of anyone within the organization. Provide a summary of financial projections for the next three to five years, where the capital to approach the market is coming from, and how it is going to be used.

Business History

In your business history section, include when the business was founded, its progress, a brief description of the founders, and the type of organization of the business, meaning whether it is a sole proprietorship, partnership, corporation, or limited liability company. State who makes decisions and why.

If yours is a new business with no history, describe your personal or professional background and experience that relate to the business. If a prospective investor is your target, show why the new business has a chance of becoming successful.

The Product Analysis

In your product analysis, explain precisely what the product is and why it is better than the competition's. Explain how the product came to be and whether any other products are on the drawing board. It would be a good idea to detail production stages and costs. Answer questions like:

- Is the product difficult to make?
- Is a skilled labor force required?
- Do you intend to use contract labor or hire your own employees?
- Where are the suppliers located, and are there additional suppliers in your area in the event your source goes out of business?

In addition, explain in detail any patents, trademarks, or copyrights; packaging designs; research and development costs still outstanding; special equipment needed; and any pending or received approvals, such as Underwriters Laboratories (UL) or factory mutual (FM) labels.

The Market Analysis

This is where you really need to shine. Include a comprehensive description of your present market, if any, and any market research that is available. Include your forecast for sales and your intended sales approach. Define who your customers are, and a five-year buying pattern.

Consider these questions.

- How will you distribute to the market?
- What has been done to test the market?
- Are there any liabilities?
- Is the product guaranteed and what insurance is required to sell it?

The marketing section of your business plan should be detailed and researched; without a useable marketing plan, the potential of your business can appear weak.

Provide information on channels of distribution; a sales compensation plan, for example who gets what percentage to ensure sales; your pricing strategy and its comparison with others; promotional concepts; and advertising and its cost. Explain how you intend to monitor the market and stay ahead of it.

The Competition Analysis

It is important to know who you are going up against. Have you researched the strengths and weaknesses of your competition? Include literature on competitors' ads in the business plan; use graphs or charts to show their weaknesses.

Be realistic. Don't assume your new product can compete as well as you would like. Anticipate problems, and be honest about how your product measures up against the competition.

The Manufacturing Report

Start this section off by describing your experience in manufacturing. Then answer some of the following questions:

- Are you making the product yourself?
- Is it being privately labeled or is it being "shopped out"?
- How is quality control guaranteed?
- What are future projections if sales rise?

The Operation Management Analysis

Describe your directors, officers, and employees, if any. Include resumés, job descriptions of key personnel, and compensation paid to each of these individuals. Include as many strong points as possible about you and your team. Indicate if you plan to use any consultants, accountants, attorneys, or bankers.

The Financial Projections

Your financial projection is important to a prospective investor because it indicates how much money you need and when you need it. It also tells the investor when she will be paid back. At a minimum, you should include a balance sheet, profit and loss statement, expected source and application of funds, profit and loss projections, and a cash-flow projection. You should, if possible, include either five years of history or three to five years of projections. Obviously, the financial projections must tie to data included elsewhere in your business plan.

Other Sections of a Business Plan

Additional information for an ideal business plan would include an:

- Evaluation of management experience and capability;
- Evaluation of the choice of the legal form of business;
- Outline of personnel policy;
- Outline of your recordkeeping system;
- Review of the risk and plans to cope with unexpected problems; and
- Pricing philosophy.

Also include your merchandising plan, credit policy, space layout plan, estimate of break-even sales based on profit projections, and even an opening-day balance sheet.

Your business plan will serve two important purposes. It will guide your actions and those on your team, and it will persuade prospective investors that you have a concept that merits serious consideration.

Business Plan Resources

Researching and writing your own business plan is highly recommended since it will make you investigate all aspects of your idea and business. However, always consider working with a business professional and consultant to ensure your business plan is accurate and well done. To enhance your ability to do your own business plan, read *The Successful Business Plan: Secrets & Strategies* by Rhonda Abrams. This book is a start-to-finish guide for writing a business plan and takes you step-by-step from your initial concept to your completed business plan. It includes tips on how to find funding sources; business plan secrets from heads of successful companies; and the Abrams Method of Flow-Through Financials to help take the mystery out of financial reports and projections. The book is available in any bookstore, or you can order the book directly from the publisher.

The Oasis Press/PSI Research
300 North Valley Drive
Grants Pass, OR 97526
(541) 479-9464
(800) 228-2275 (Nationwide)

Funding Sources

There are various sources from which you can obtain capital, and while each has its own benefits and faults, many times, it is your particular situation that will warrant where you will first attempt to obtain start-up money or investment capital. Here is an overview of the different means available.

Family, Friends, and Savings

In the earliest stages of development, you may find it easier to obtain financial assistance from family or friends. Often, you will use your personal savings to get started. Later, an investor may take a favorable view of your project and provide additional funding. Your investment, of course, contains the risk that you may lose your money and end up deeply in debt to family and friends. Keep in mind, nothing ruins solid relationships faster than owing debts to others.

Banks

While most banks will not lend to new ventures, some are willing to lend money to small businesses to finance fixed assets, inventories, and accounts receivable where substantial collateral is available. Some banks even have venture capital subsidiaries that operate in essentially the same manner as private venture capital firms.

SBA Lending Programs

If you need to borrow money for your business and cannot obtain regular bank financing, don't overlook the possibility of obtaining a loan through the U.S. Small Business Administration (SBA). The SBA provides financing to small business through direct loans or loan guarantees made to private lending institutions. To obtain a list of local banks that are approved SBA centers, visit the library or consult your local telephone directory for the phone number of the local SBA office. You could also contact the SBA Answer Desk, which offers a wide array of prerecorded informational messages on SBA programs and services.

SBA Answer Desk
(800) 827-5722

SBIR Grant Program

One good way to receive funds for new idea development is when the idea also serves a need for the government. Through the SBA's Office of Innovation, Research and Technology, you can receive Small Business Innovation Research (SBIR) pre-solicitation announcements. If you qualify as a small business, you can receive grants for research and development through the U.S. Department of Defense, Department of Commerce, Department of Energy, Department of Health and Human Services, or the Environmental Protection Agency. In general, the solicitation includes a list of problems that these federal agencies wish to solve, and allows you to submit a proposal for researching the solution.

The three-phase program grants up to $50,000 in the first phase, up to $500,000 in the second phase, and phase three is conducted by nonfederal funds to take the solution to commercial applications. The national SBIR program is considered to be the world's largest research and development market. Awards are made for research in many different fields, including but not limited to, manufacturing, environmental, life sciences, avionics, lasers, communications, software, optical computing, aquaculture, educational materials, energy, and electronics. The following programs offer funds to any company with 500 or fewer employees for conducting research and development on the nation's most pressing scientific and engineering problems:

- The Advanced Technology Program (ATP) of the National Institute for Standards and Technology funds high-risk industrial research and development with significant potential for stimulating economic growth and improving U.S. competitiveness. Single company applicants can receive up to $2 million over a three-year period. More than $400 million SBIR awards are made to the ATP.
- The Energy Related Invention Program (ERIP) evaluates and funds non-nuclear energy technologies by small companies and individuals that are ready to be moved into the market. More than $5 million for grants and services are awarded.
- The Environmental Technology Initiative (ETI) of the Environmental Protection Agency supports technology projects in Global Climate Change. Seventy-five million dollars, plus $5 million for commercialization of technology are awarded to this program.
- The Small Business Technology Transfer Research Program (STTR) is modeled on SBIR and funds joint proposals that bring together the entrepreneurial talent of high-tech small business with the innovative ideas of scientists and engineers at university, federally funded research, and development centers, as well as nonprofit research institutions. More than $900 million SBIR awards are made by all major federal agencies to this program.
- The Technology Reinvestment Project (TRP) supports development of defense technology, which also has commercial applications. More than $635 million SBIR awards are made to the TRP.

Sources of information regarding SBIR grants include:

Allied Technology Group, Inc.
4200 Forbes Blvd., Suite 106
Lanham, MD 20706-4342

This group is the Program Support Office for NASA.

The Innovation Development Institute
45 Beach Bluff Avenue, Suite 300
Swampscott, MA 01907-0195
(617) 595-2920

This institute offers a newsletter entitled, *Inknowvation*, telephone information services, and orientation seminars.

Peat, Marwick, Main and Company
700 First Oklahoma Tower
Oklahoma City, OK 73102
(405) 239-6411

This company offers a concise proposal-writing booklet entitled, *Small Business Innovation Research Grants: How to Obtain Them to Finance Your Ideas.* Consulting services are also provided for a fee.

Sandra Conn Associates, Inc.
2551 North Clark Street, Suite 400
Chicago, IL 60614-1717
(312) 327-0082

This company publishes a proposal writing book entitled, *Writing SBIR Proposals*, plus offers orientation and proposal-writing seminars.

The Small Business High Technology Institute
3300 North Central Avenue, Suite 1700
Phoenix, AZ 85012
(602) 277-6603

This institute provides a report to the states and a collection of successful Phase 1 proposals.

For further information on the SBIR grant program and to be included on the government's mailing list, contact:

Office of Innovation, Research and Technology
U.S. Small Business Administration
409 3rd Street, SW, Suite 4000
Washington, DC 20416
(202) 205-6770 (in Washington, DC)
(817) 855-6500 (in Ft. Worth, Texas)
FAX (202) 205-7064

SBA Online Bulletin Board
(800) 697-4636 (via modem)

SBA on the Internet
http://www.sbaonline.sba.gov

NASA/SBIR Electronic Bulletin Board
(800) 547-1811 (via modem)

Private or Exempt Public Offerings

While public offerings are an unlikely source for immediate start-up capital, a company in an expansion phase may be able to raise capital for promoting new products without fully registering its offering with the Securities and Exchange Commission (SEC) or similar state commissions. One should consider such factors as lag time between initiation and actual financing, and the complexities of having private shareholders.

Registered Public Offering

A full-scale registration with the SEC and state authorities may be required when seeking larger amounts of capital. As with private placements, most small ventures will not view public offerings as an attractive financing source due to the time, cost, and registration requirements involved.

Venture Capitalists

Venture capital firms are usually privately owned or formed as general or limited partnerships, composed primarily of institutional investors or wealthy individuals. Most venture capital firms will seek investments in which they expect to realize a high rate of return — many times ten-to-one or higher.

Whatever source of funding you choose will depend largely upon your own situation and knowledge or background. One consideration which may be overlooked is the importance of understanding your state and federal securities laws on fund-raising efforts. When dealing with friends and relatives, an inventor may forget that any efforts to raise capital require compliance with state and federal securities laws. Check with your legal adviser.

Some sources for finding venture capital include:

Office of Energy-Related Inventions – OERI
National Bureau of Standards
U.S. Department of Commerce
Gaithersburg, MD 20899
(202) 586-5000
FAX (202) 586-5049

The OERI provides grants for research and development.

National Assoc. of Small Business Investment Companies – NASBIC
618 Washington Building, NW
Washington, DC 20005
(202) 638-3411

The NASBIC will provide companies with possible investors.

National Science Foundation – NSF
4701 Wilson Blvd., Room 590
Arlington, VA 22230
(703) 306-1391
FAX (703) 306-0337

The NSF provides federal research and development funding.

National Venture Capital Assoc. – NVCA
1225 19th Street NW, Suite 750
Washington, DC 20036
(202) 659-5756

The NVCA will assist in finding the right kind of investor for you.

Venture Capital Exchange
Enterprise Development Center
University of Tulsa
600 South College
Tulsa, OK 74104
(918) 631-2684

This company will evaluate your idea and help finance — for a fee.

Starting Your Own Business

Going into business to manufacture and sell your product is a major undertaking that involves more time, money, and energy than most people imagine. It is also very risky. Every new enterprise begins with optimism and enthusiasm, but less than 25 percent survive the first year. Many more go out of business the second year, and yet the few that do succeed and grow become an inspiration to future entrepreneurs. It takes dedication and diligence. Starting and operating a business will involve, at the minimum, decisions on organizational options, management style, accounting techniques, marketing approach, legal and tax fundamentals, insurance planning, and many other considerations.

Just filling out the tax forms alone can make many would-be business-people think twice! But, if you consider these matters as only part of the adventure, your dedication will generally pay off.

The bookstores are full of business books that discuss various aspects of starting and operating a business, but there is one unique publication you may wish to read before opening your doors — *Start Your Business: A Beginner's Guide*, 2nd ed., by The Oasis Press. This easy-to-follow book covers the many "to-do's" and decisions you will need to handle before your opening day. It discusses start-up requirements, money matters, marketing, production, business plan writing, and much more. At the end of each section, you will have a plan of action on a particular topic, making you better informed and prepared for the challenge that lies ahead. For more information, contact:

The Oasis Press/PSI Research
300 North Valley Drive
Grants Pass, OR 97526
(541) 479-9464
(800) 228-2275 (Nationwide)

Incubators

If you wish to start your own business, and promote and manufacture your own product, consider a business incubator.

The small business incubator is an increasingly popular and innovative economic development tool to improve the success rate of new firms. An incubator is a building or group of buildings in which a number of new or growing businesses can locate and operate with much lower overhead cost than in a conventional space where rent would be much higher.

Incubator facilities are characterized by access to shared, centralized services such as clerical and administrative help, receiving and shipping facilities, conference rooms, computers, fax and copy machines, and assistance. Because the incubator is designed to promote the development of small businesses, it provides low-cost space, business counseling and training, and a co-op environment offering expertise and information to its tenants.

Many of the 200-plus incubator projects across the nation have been sponsored by private corporations interested in new product development and services. Many small companies starting out in an incubator get that extra edge to help them survive the first few years when mistakes can be all too costly.

The SBA's Division of Management Assistance sponsors nationwide assistance programs, including the Small Business Development Center (SBDC) program for small businesses. There are more than 500 universities and colleges participating in this program. By calling the toll-free number below, you may find that using an adviser is to your benefit. They may be contacted at:

Division of Management Assistance
U.S. Small Business Administration
409 3rd Street, SW, Suite 4000
Washington, DC 20416
(202) 205-6450 (General information)

National Business Incubator Assoc. – NBIA
20 East Circle, Suite 190
Athens, OH 45701
(614) 593-4331

Notes

8

Know the Licensing Process

Common sense is genius dressed in its working clothes. — Ralph Waldo Emerson

Licensing Rewards

Your invention's evolution — from concept to market — involves substantial time, money, and effort. You are responsible for taking an idea and turning it into something of value, and you may look to licensing to reward your efforts.

The first step in licensing is, of course, finding someone who is interested in your idea or product. Finding a licensee is much like many of the other steps in developing your idea. You must decide what you want, research your prospects, then go after it. Your chance of licensing your idea will depend greatly upon how well you have completed the development and marketing of your product or idea.

If you are presently marketing your idea, even in a limited fashion, your idea has much greater merit, and you may have had inquiries already from your competitors about licensing arrangements.

The best place to start looking for a licensee is within the same industry as your product. The *Thomas Register* is an excellent source for finding such names. Generally, the process of writing letters to prospective licensees can take time. If you have not done any marketing, it may be time to start publicizing that your product is up for license, as well as approaching your business contacts.

Local chambers of commerce and business support centers will also provide leads. Contacting local venture capitalists or banks can also provide possibilities; however, local non-professional interests are generally much easier to deal with.

Remember, industry needs new products. It is a matter of being seen by those seeking something innovative. It is usually at this point inventors are at their most vulnerable. Be careful in thinking that the first interested party will be your last. As the inventor, you probably feel as though you have come too far to miss the boat now, and you may make a hasty decision in signing a contract, just to say you have done it. Try not to get too excited, feeling as though you are lucky just to have someone talking to you. On the other hand, realize it is the licensee who is taking the risk and adjust accordingly.

Preliminary Considerations

Before finding a prospective licensee or going to the table to negotiate a licensing agreement, be sure you know what you want. Many inventors find license negotiations very intimidating and may lose certain bargaining points because of their inexperience.

Before any negotiating takes place, consider these points.

- Involvement — Do you want or need to be involved after the deal is signed?
- Legal assistance — A lawyer may be well worth the expense during negotiations.
- Royalty percentage -— Five percent is generally a good starting point for the inventor receiving up-front money as well.
- Trust — Do you really trust the company you are dealing with? Research its background before deciding.
- Up-front money — This can be a strong bargaining point and possible trade-off potential for higher royalties.

Find a Licensee

If you have a truly unique product, licensing can be as simple as going to the store aisles where your competitors' products are found. Companies are always eager to expand their product lines into new areas, or to sell improved versions of currently available products. Nearly every package gives the name and location of its producer.

After visiting the store, go to the library and become familiar with the sources available for research. The best sources for investigating licensing include:

- *Dun & Bradstreet's Reference Book of Corporate Management.* This book gives a detailed biographical description of more than 75,000 principal officers of more than 12,000 leading companies. It supplies names, titles, and an array of vital statistics.
- *Standard & Poor's Register of Corporations, Directors and Executives.* This publication lists 45,000 corporations, along with their executives, and detailed information on some 450,000 potential licensee contacts.

Other good sources are the *Million Dollar Directory* and the *Middle Market Directory*, both from Dun & Bradstreet, listing thousands of companies, each with assets exceeding $500,000.

It is important to note that communications with a potential licensee should be directed to top management — the president or chief executive officer. Although letters are many times first screened by secretaries, professional-looking communications will almost always draw attention to you and your product.

You will, unfortunately, receive your share of we-are-not-interested letters. But for now, just put them aside for future reference.

Meet with a Potential Licensee

A successful first meeting with a potential licensee is crucial to your licensing effort. You are not only promoting your product, you are also promoting yourself as knowledgeable and professional. Here are some points you should be prepared to cover.

- Describe the demand for the product and how you know about the demand. Include market research and testing.
- Discuss all the applications and alternatives to the product.
- Demonstrate why the licensee will benefit from your product, and discuss the products presently on the market.
- Discuss potential patents, trademarks, and copyrights.
- Explain your qualifications for inventing the product, emphasizing your business background.

Evaluate Your Contract

A sound licensing agreement will benefit both you and the licensee, but it is only as good as the integrity of those who sign it. Don't forget to read the fine print — if it looks too good to be true, it usually is.

While negotiating a licensing agreement for your invention, it pays to stay cool and view things from all possible angles. Taking time to think now will help you avoid licensing what could result in a future lawsuit. Litigation could take years to be settled and it will cost you more than is imaginable before you recover any money, if ever.

Because licensing agreements are very complex, only a few legal considerations of licensing are discussed here. It is always advisable to look into local and state restrictions when signing any legal document. Many inventors will fall into unfamiliar territory when negotiating a license and could fail to follow local or state antitrust and securities laws. Obtain legal counsel when getting ready to sign on the dotted line.

Glossary of Terms Used in Contracts and Licenses

To help you better understand contracts and licensing agreements, as well as to help you work more effectively with your legal adviser, become familiar with the legal definitions of terms commonly used in licensing and contracts. Understanding these terms may help you protect your ideas and avoid lawsuits later.

Derivative works. This refers to any refinement or modification to your product. If not properly defined, an improvement on your product could allow the licensee to license the product and not you! Many contracts are weak in this area, and it is your responsibility to assure that any product improvement made by others is included in your product and that the altered product remains your property.

Exclusivity. National or even worldwide exclusivity rights can be a strong negotiating position and should not be bargained away easily. Use exclusivity as a bargaining chip and remember, if you found one licensee, you can find more.

Gross profits. This is the net sales price less the cost of raw materials, labor, manufacturing, shipping, and packaging. Many different costs may be subtracted from the gross profits. Be very careful about labor cost, because a manufacturer or investor can take back all that he invested in the product and take a tax write-off. This costing must be defined and controlled now, or your royalties may pay the investor's brother $100,000 a year to box the product.

Licensed devices. This explains exactly what the invention consists of and limits the scope of the agreement to only that product. Look to the future; you may be in another business later and may want to license to another industry.

Licensed patents. This includes the patent number and claims, or gives an explanation beyond that detailed under licensed devices. If a patent is pending, detail what happens if you are not granted a patent, because it could happen.

Minimum royalty. This details the minimum amount of royalty you will receive at certain intervals. It should say you will get paid, no matter what problems the licensee may encounter.

Payment. Detail how much is paid to you and to others, and when. It should include a late penalty and a time limit for payments or royalties, and should detail what happens when payments are not met. In addition, include a cut-off point for late payments where all rights revert back to you and a statement that any partial payments are nonrefundable.

Performance clause. This could be the most important definition included in your licensing agreement. A performance clause will simply state a minimum number of units which should be sold within a specified period of time. It works well as an "anti-shelving" clause and it should explain in detail what happens if sales expectation is not met. The anti-shelving clause is a means of keeping interest in your product, as the licensee will be paying royalties to you even if the product never reaches the market. After a certain time, all rights should revert back to you. If this is not clearly set out in writing, you will have to go to court to win back your invention.

Records and reports. Define the type of records to be kept, and also allow for an independent audit, which helps keep everyone honest. It should also indicate whether the investor is entitled to review records, which can be important in estimating royalties.

Research and development (R&D). This defines the effort to stay ahead of the competition and should even include fees to be paid to the inventor for further research.

Sublicensing. This can be a quick way for the inventor to lose all control if not restricted by the original contract. If the contract does not restrict sublicensing, you could find yourself competing with your own product shipped from another country.

Term. This is the amount of time the license will run.

Termination and abandonment. This specifies what happens if everything falls through. Make sure that in a licensing agreement you have no responsibility to pay back company loans. State clearly that you receive all rights to improvements should the contract fail.

Third-party infringement. This can cause much hardship and it must be detailed as to who fights the lawsuits. The licensee will consider it the inventor's problem, yet the business could fail if the inventor is poorly financed. Be careful of the wording.

Up-front payment. Negotiating for up-front money will depend largely upon the product and how badly the licensee wants it. The licensee may argue that he or she has to invest in molds, engineering, testing, and start up. Your argument, of course, is that the money is required to reimburse out-of-pocket expenses for development, prototyping, patenting, and other costs. Additionally, up-front money will sometimes make the licensee work a little harder to recoup his or her investment.

Licensing Guidelines

To find out more about the licensing process, contact:

Licensing Industry Merchandizers Association
200 Park Avenue, Suite 303E
New York, NY 10166

The License Agreement

The license agreement example on the following pages shows a contract that favors the inventor. It may help you when comparing other agreements that may lean more toward the licensee.

This contract example is meant solely to be used as a guide. As with the tax laws, state and federal securities laws, and other laws which impact on business, licensing may be subject to state and federal franchise laws, antitrust laws, and case law. To be safe, check with your legal adviser before entering into any licensing agreement.

License Agreement – Sample

This agreement is made between

____ ("Licensor") and

____ ("Licensee")

on ____________, 19 ____. Licensor is the sole inventor and owner of

_____________________________________ ("Intellectual Property")

including but not limited to certain information, technical data, processes, know-how, stop practices, drawings, plans, specifications, methods of manufacture, trademarks, and other data hereinafter known as the invention. Licensee desires to obtain a nonexclusive license to utilize the information and to manufacture and sell the invention. In consideration of the mutual promises in this agreement, the parties agree as follows and defined herein:

1. Scope. This agreement shall be limited to the product and information known as the invention.
2. License. Subject to the terms of this agreement, Licensor grants to Licensee the nonexclusive, nontransferable right and license to use the information to manufacture the invention and sell or lease the invention within the United States. No license, expressed or implied, is granted to employ the information for any other purpose whatsoever.
3. Compensation.
   - A. Payment. The consideration due and payable to Licensor for the rights granted to Licensee hereunder shall be the sum of $________________________ U.S. dollars due and payable on execution of this agreement.
   - B. Further Consideration. As further consideration for the grants of this license provides for hereunder, Licensee agrees to spend no less than $____________________ for the purpose of manufacturing, distribution and promotion of the invention before 6 months from the date of execution of this agreement.
   - C. Royalties. In addition to the consideration due and payable to Licensor, Licensee agrees to assume and pay royalties on all licensed devices sold equal to ________% of the gross profits realized from the exploration and rights to the licensed invention.
   - D. Payment Schedule. After ____________, 19____. Payments of royalties shall be paid to Licensor with each quarterly report.

License Agreement – Sample

4. Records. Licensee shall maintain accurate records relating to the manufacturing and sale of the invention. Licensee shall render quarterly reports to Licensor within three weeks of the end of each quarter showing the total quantity of inventions produced; the quantity sold, leased or otherwise utilized; the gross receipts received by Licensor for such transactions; and the amounts due Licensor as royalties. Licensor or an authorized representative shall have the right to inspect and copy such records and books of account upon Licensor's written request, and such inspection and copying shall be done during Licensee's regular business hours.

5. Research and Development. Licensee shall make funds available for the further research, development and improvements and derivative works of the invention. Funds shall be no less than $_________ per year. All improvements and derivative works of the invention shall be included within this agreement.

6. Termination of the agreement.

   A. Unless terminated sooner, this agreement shall remain in force through _______________, 19______.

   B. Either party shall have the right to terminate this agreement if the other fails to perform per written agreement herein, provided that such failure shall not have been remedied by the defaulting party within sixty days of having received written notice of intention to terminate.

   C. Bankruptcy or Insolvency of Licensee shall automatically terminate this agreement with all rights returning to Licensor.

   D. Licensee shall have the right to sell or lease any products on hand or contracted for as of the date of termination. Any termination shall not release Licensee from payment of royalties accrued through the date of termination.

7. This agreement shall be interpreted in accordance with the laws of the State of _______________.

8. Licensee agrees to make adequate warning for the product, and comply with all applicable laws and regulations.

9. Licensee agrees to carry third party liability insurance to insure and adequately cover both Licensor and Licensee against claims resulting from damage or personal injury through sale or use of the product (Invention). Licensee agrees to make Licensor as an additional insured on such insurance policies.

License Agreement – Sample

10. No terms of this agreement can be modified or waived except in writing signed by both parties.
11. Service of notice as provided for in this agreement shall be given in writing and shall be considered duly served and given by mailing the same, postage prepaid by registered mail to the parties at the following addresses:

    ____

    ____

    ____

    ____

    and

    ____

    ____

    ____

    ____

12. A minimum royalty shall be paid to Licensor of $____________ per month for the first 6 months after execution of agreement and $____________ per month from 7th month on.
13. Licensee shall permit, during normal business hours, a duly authorized representative of the Licensor, or Licensor to enter Licensee premises for purpose of ascertaining that the Licensee is complying with the provisions of this agreement.
14. Nothing herein shall be construed as a warranty or representation given by Licensor to Licensee attesting to the scope or validity of the herein named patent application or any patent issuing thereon.
15. Third Party Infringement suits shall be entered into equally with Licensor monies transferred from future royalties if necessary. Said settlement shall be equally divided between Licensee and Licensor.

In witness whereof the parties hereto have hereunto signed their respective names and affixed their respective corporate seal.

____ ("Licensor")

____ ("Licensee")

Executed this ________________ day of ______________, 19 _____

Notes

Conclusion

The man who removes a mountain begins by carrying away small stones. — Chinese proverb

George Bernard Shaw said it best when he stated that the reasonable person adapts himself to the world; the unreasonable one persists in trying to adapt the world to himself. Therefore, all progress depends upon the unreasonable man.

I had to ask myself, am I an unreasonable person? I would not accept that the world could do without my new ideas. If I were to look back at the efforts that drove me on the quest for success, I would stagger. I had to believe in the impossible; I had to do what had never been done; I had a dream, and I had to see it through. I would have it no other way.

When I started out, I had no knowledge of patents, trademarks, and copyrights, and now I own all three. When I could not afford to file for a patent, I learned to write my own. I built and tested prototypes in my garage and spent weekends and nights at the library. I learned about marketing, financing, and licensing by rolling up my sleeves and getting to work on what I knew had to be done. And when it was all said and done, I signed my first license agreement for $500,000 knowing full well that I had earned it. That, however, was just the beginning. My first invention led me to a Department of Defense (DOD) grant which led me to my first book, which led me to a Department of Energy (DOE) grant, which led me on and on and on.

In short, there is no conclusion for the unreasonable man or woman. There are only dreams to be realized and new ideas to be nurtured and developed.

A

Information Sources for Inventors

This appendix features a state-by-state listing of where you can go for more assistance and information on developing and marketing your business idea. These lists feature a variety of private organizations, as well as a variety of governmental agencies, you may contact. Whenever possible, fax numbers have been included for your convenience.

The addresses themselves are arranged in alphabetical order according to organization or program title; however, each state's list begins with its Small Business Development Center's (SBDC's) state office. SBDCs are valuable resources for the beginning entrepreneur because they offer free business counseling, training, and referrals. Each state has several SBDC locations; contact your state's SBDC office to find the SBDC nearest you.

In addition to SBDCs, many of the lists feature addresses for venture capitalists, patent consultants, technology centers, and inventors' organizations. If you don't find an inventors' organization for your state, you can research an updated list of state inventors' organizations at your local library.

Finally, if you are interested in exploring opportunities in the global marketplace, you will find a listing of foreign country organizations at the end of this appendix.

ALABAMA

Alabama SBDC Consortium
University of Alabama
1717 11th Avenue, Suite 419
Birmingham, AL 35294-4410
(205) 934-7260
FAX (205) 934-7645

Alabama Technology Assistance Program
1717 11th Avenue, South, Suite 419
Birmingham, AL 35294
(205) 934-7260
FAX (205) 934-7645

Office for the Advancement of Developing Industries
University of Alabama
1075 13th Street, South
Birmingham, AL 35294-4440
(205) 934-2190
FAX (205) 934-1037

U.S. Small Business Administration
Attn. Business Development Office
2121 Eighth Avenue, North, Suite 200
Birmingham, AL 35203-2398
(205) 731-1338
FAX (205) 731-1404

ALASKA

Alaska SBDC
University of Alaska
430 West 7th Avenue, Suite 110
Anchorage, AK 99501
(907) 274-7232
FAX (907) 274-9524

Alaska Inventors & Entrepreneurs Assoc., Inc.
P.O. Box 241801
Anchorage, AK 99524-1801
(907) 276-4337
FAX (907) 278-2982

Alaska Science/Technology Foundation
550 West 7th Avenue, Suite 360
Anchorage, AK 99501
(907) 272-4333
FAX (907) 274-6228

Economic Development District, Inc.
110 South Willow, Suite 106
Kenai, AK 99611
(907) 283-3335
FAX (907) 283-3913

Inventors' Institute of Alaska
P.O. Box 876154
Wasilla, AK 99687
(907) 376-5114

World Trade Center – Alaska
421 West First Avenue, Suite 300
Anchorage, AK 99501
(907) 278-7233
FAX (907) 278-2982

Z.J. Loussac Public Library
Serials/Acquisitions Department
3600 Denali Street
Anchorage, AK 99503-6093
(907) 261-2970
FAX (907) 562-1244

ARIZONA

Arizona SBDC Network
2411 West 14th Street, Suite 132
Tempe, AZ 85281
(602) 731-8720
FAX (602) 731-8729

Arizona State Research Institute
Arizona State University
Tempe, AZ 85287
(602) 965-9011
FAX (602) 965-2012

Arizona Technology Incubator
1535 North Hayden Road
Scottsdale, AZ 85257-3773
(602) 990-0400
FAX (602) 970-6355

Engineering Professional Development
University of Arizona
Harvill Building, Box 9
Tucson, AZ 85721
(602) 621-5104
FAX (602) 621-1443

Innovation Development Corp.
408 West Forest Avenue
Flagstaff, AZ 86001
(708) 891-0316

Office of Technology Transfer
University of Arizona
1430 East Fort Lowell Road, Suite 200
Tucson, AZ 85719-2366
(602) 621-5000
FAX (602) 322-0846

Synergetics
3860 West First
P.O. Box 809
Thatcher, AZ 85552
(602) 428-4073

ARKANSAS

Arkansas SBDC
University of Arkansas at Little Rock
100 South Main, Suite 401
Little Rock, AR 72201
(501) 324-9043
FAX (501) 324-9049

Eastern Arkansas Business Incubator System
5501 Krueger Drive
Jonesboro, AR 72401
(501) 935-8365
FAX (501) 931-5133

Entrepreneurial Service Center
University of Arkansas at Fayetteville
BA 443
Fayetteville, AR 72701
(501) 575-7227
FAX (501) 575-7446

Inventors' Congress, Inc.
P.O. Box 411
Dardanelle, AR 72834
(501) 229-4515

CALIFORNIA

California SBDC Program
Department of Commerce
801 K Street, Suite 1700
Sacramento, CA 95814
(916) 324-5068
FAX (916) 322-5084

American Innovation Assoc. – AIA
P.O. Box 1107
Oak View, CA 93022
(805) 649-1046
FAX (805) 649-5264

American Inventor Network
6770 Depot Street
Sebastopol, CA 95472
(707) 823-3865
FAX (707) 823-0913

Ames Technology Commercialization Center
National Aeronautics & Space Administration
155-A Moffett Park Drive, Suite 104
Sunnyvale, CA 94089
(408) 734-4700
FAX (408) 734-4946

Asian Inventor Entrepreneur Cooperative
18325 Malden Street
Northridge, CA 91325-3585
(818) 882-4506

Black Inventors' Technical Resources
P.O. Box 6402
Torrance, CA 90504
(310) 323-4668
FAX (310) 323-4668

Bureau of Business Research and Service
California State University
Fresno, CA 93740
(510) 881-3805

Center For New Venture Alliance
California State University
Hayward, CA 94542-3066
(510) 881-3805
FAX (510) 727-2039

CONNECT/Program in Technology and Entrepreneurship
University of California – San Diego
La Jolla, CA 92093-0176
(619) 534-6114
FAX (619) 552-0649

Cossman International, Inc.
P.O. Box 4480
Palm Springs, CA 92263
(619) 320-7717
FAX (619) 320-9247

Far West Regional Technology Transfer Center
National Aeronautics & Space Administration
3716 South Hope Street, Room 200
Los Angeles, CA 90007
(213) 743-6132
FAX (213) 746-9043

Idea to Market Network
P.O. Box 12248
Santa Rosa, CA 95406
(800) ITM-3210
FAX (707) 584-4161

Innovation Center
Stanford University
Stanford, CA 94305
(415) 723-2300

Institute of Entrepreneurship
California State University
5151 State University
Los Angeles, CA 90032
(213) 343-2971

Invention Services International Corp.
P.O. Box 93669
Los Angeles, CA 90093-0669
(800) 458-5624
FAX (213) 962-8588

Inventive Product Development
Margolin Development Company
P.O. Box 2846
Newport Beach, CA 92663
(714) 645-5950
FAX (714) 645-5974

Inventors' Assistance League
345 West Cypress Street
Glendale, CA 91204
(818) 246-6541

Inventors' Assoc., Inc. – Central Valley
P.O. Box 1551
Manteca, CA 95336
(209) 239-5414

Inventors' Guild of America
1852 Kirby Road
Glendale, CA 91208
(818) 507-0263

Inventors Helper Industries
4480 Treat Blvd., Suite 310
Concord, CA 94521
(510) 676-4975
FAX (510) 535-0450

Inventors New Venture Alliance
P.O. Box 371148
Montara, CA 94037
(510) 726-1945

Inventors' Workshop
International Education Foundation
7332 Mason Avenue
Canoga Park, CA 91306-2822
(818) 340-4268
FAX (818) 884-8312

Inventors' Workshop Internat'l. Education Fdtn. – IWIEF
Antelope Valley Chapter
4444 East Avenue R, Space 127
Palmdale, CA 93550
(805) 273-0144

Inventors' Workshop Internat'l. Education Fdtn. – IWIEF
Santa Cruz Chapter
730 Encino Drive
Aptos, CA 95003
(408) 662-1936

ISTAR, Inc.
406 Alta Avenue
Santa Monica, CA 90402-2714
(310) 394-7332

The James F. Riordan Co., Inc.
3110 Camerosa Circle
Cameron Park, CA 95682
(916) 676-4729

Macro-Search Corp.
2082 Business Center Drive, Suite 225
Irvine, CA 92715
(714) 253-9930
FAX (714) 253-0951

Pennie & Edmonds
2730 Sand Hill Road
Menlo Park, CA 94025
(415) 854-3660
FAX (415) 854-3694

Pillsbury, Madison & Sutro
Ten Almaden Blvd., Suite 800
San Jose, CA 95113-2266
(408) 977-0120
FAX (408) 977-0129

San Diego Inventors Group
11190 Poblado Road
San Diego, CA 92127
(619) 673-4733
FAX (619) 451-6154

Sawyer Inventive Resource Center
520 Mendocino Avenue, Suite 210
Santa Rosa, CA 95401
(707) 524-1773
FAX (707) 524-1772

Small Entity Patent Owners Assoc.
295 Stevenson Drive
Pleasant Hill, CA 94523
(510) 934-1331
FAX (510) 934-1132

Technology Properties, Ltd.
4010 Moorpark Avenue, Suite 215
San Jose, CA 95117
(408) 243-9898
FAX (408) 296-6637

Total Multimedia
299 West Hillcrest Drive, Suite 200
Thousand Oaks, CA 91360
(805) 497-4053

COLORADO

Colorado SBDC
Colorado Office of Business Development
1625 Broadway, Suite 1710
Denver, CO 80202
(303) 892-3809
FAX (303) 892-3848

Affiliated Inventors' Foundation, Inc.
902 North Circle Drive, Suite 208
Colorado Springs, CO 80909-5002
(719) 635-1234
FAX (719) 635-1578

Business Advancement Centers
Colorado University
335 South 43rd Street
Boulder, CO 80303
(303) 499-8114

Colorado Biomedical Venture Center
1610 Pierce Street
Denver, CO 80214
(303) 237-3998
FAX (303) 237-4010

Colorado Inventors' Council, Inc.
P.O. Box 88
Holyoke, CO 80734
(303) 854-3851

Colorado School of Mines
Department of Chemistry &
Geochemistry
Golden, CO 80801
(303) 273-3626
FAX (303) 273-3629

Dakin Law Technology, LLC.
384 Iverness Drive, South, Suite 205
Englewood, CO 80112
(303) 779-1992
FAX (303) 779-9784

National Inventors' Assoc.
P.O. Box 2032
Littleton, CO 80161
(303) 755-1456

Rocky Mountain Inventors' Congress
P.O. Box 4365
Denver, CO 80204
(303) 758-6757

CONNECTICUT

Connecticut SBDC
University of Connecticut
2 Bourn Place, U-94
Storrs, CT 06269-5094
(203) 486-4135
FAX (203) 486-1576

Innovators' Network of Greater Danbury
37 Seneca Road
Danbury, CT 06811
(203) 797-8955

InoNet, Inc.
187 South Salem Road
Ridgefield, CT 06877
(203) 438-1661
FAX (203) 221-7060

Patent & Licensing Group of New England
10 Bay Street, Suite 112
Westport, CT 06880
(203) 454-3540
FAX (203) 222-8608

SIMCO, Inc.
61 River Road
Weston, CT 06883
(203) 227-0041
FAX (203) 222-1890

Technology Assistance Center
Connecticut Innovations, Inc.
845 Brook Street
Rocky Hill, CT 06067
(203) 258-4305

DELAWARE

Delaware SBDC
University of Delaware
Purnell Hall, Suite 005
Newark, DE 19716-2711
(302) 831-2747
FAX (302) 831-1423

Delaware Economic Development Office
99 Kings Highway
P.O. Box 1401
Dover, DE 19903
(302) 739-4271
FAX (302) 739-5749

DISTRICT OF COLUMBIA

District of Columbia SBDC
Howard University
2600 6th Street, NW, Room 128
Washington, DC 20059
(202) 806-1550
FAX (202) 806-1777

Innovation Information Center
George Washington University
2130 H Street, NW
Washington, DC 20052
(202) 994-1000

Intellectual Property Owners Assoc.
1255 23rd Street, NW, Suite 850
Washington, DC 20037
(202) 466-2396
FAX (202) 466-2893

U.S. Department of Energy
1000 Independence Avenue
CE 521, 5E052
Washington, DC 20585
(202) 586-1478
FAX (202) 586-8134

U.S. Patent and Trademark Office
U.S. Department of Commerce
Washington, DC 20231
(703) 308-0975
FAX (703) 305-3463

U.S. Small Business Administration
409 3rd Street, SW, Suite 4000
Washington, DC 20416
(202) 205-6770
FAX (202) 205-7064

FLORIDA

Florida SBDC Network
University of West Florida
19 West Garden Street, Suite 300
Pensacola, FL 32501
(904) 444-2060
FAX (904) 444-2070

Center for Health Technologies, Inc.
1150 NW 14th Street, Suite 105
Miami, FL 33136-2112
(305) 325-2733
FAX (305) 325-2698

Edison Inventors' Assoc., Inc.
P.O. Box 07398
Fort Myers, FL 33919
(813) 275-4332

The Enterprise Corp. of Tampa Bay
1111 North Westshore Blvd., Suite 200-B
Tampa, FL 33607
(813) 288-0445
FAX (813) 554-2356

Florida Department of Commerce
Attn. Research Economist
107 West Gaines Street
Tallahassee, FL 32399-2000
(904) 487-3134
FAX (904) 487-6516

Florida Product Innovation Center
2622 NW 43rd Street, Suite B3
Gainsville, FL 32606-7428
(904) 334-1680
FAX (904) 334-1682

The Inventor's Club
WSRE-TV
1000 College Blvd.
Pensacola, FL 32504
(904) 484-1224
FAX (904) 484-1255

Inventors' Society of South Florida
P.O. Box 4306
Boynton Beach, FL 33424
(407) 736-6594

Klenner International
P.O. Box 1748
Ormond Beach, FL 32175
(904) 673-4339
FAX (904) 673-5911

Product Center Corp.
4001 NW 97th Avenue
Miami, FL 33178
(305) 592-7260
FAX (305) 592-7937

PSPI, Inc.
Attn. Tech Specialist
15 Dahoon Court, South
Homosassa, FL 34446-8922
(904) 382-1535

Tampa Bay Inventors' Council
P.O. Box 2254
Largo, FL 34646
(813) 391-0315

Thermal Storage Systems, Inc.
2517 Trinidad Street
Sarasota, FL 34231
(813) 921-0517

Tutle/International Technology Marketing
2601 Seabreeze Court
Orlando, FL 32805
(407) 423-8016
FAX (407) 291-1176

GEORGIA

Georgia SBDC
University of Georgia
1180 East Broad Street
Athens, GA 30602-5412
(706) 542-6804
FAX (706) 542-6776

CAN DO Industries, Inc.
7610 Ball Mill Road
Atlanta, GA 30350
(404) 396-1401
FAX (404) 671-1070

Georgia Institute of Technology
Library and Information Center
Atlanta, GA 30332-0900
(404) 894-4508
FAX (404) 894-8190

Inventors' Clubs of America, Inc.
P.O. Box 450261
Atlanta, GA 31145-0261
(800) 336-0169
FAX (404) 355-8889

U.S. Department of Energy
Atlanta Support Office
730 Peachtree Street, NE, Suite 876
Atlanta, GA 30308
(404) 347-7139
FAX (404) 347-3098

HAWAII

Hawaii SBDC Network
University of Hawaii at Hilo
200 West Kiwili
Hilo, HI 96720-4091
(808) 933-3515
FAX (808) 933-3683

Inventors' Council of Hawaii
P.O. Box 27844
Honolulu, HI 96287
(808) 595-4296

Statewide Strategy for High Technology Growth
High Technology Development Corp.
300 Kahelu Avenue, Suite 35
Honolulu, HI 96789
(808) 625-5293
FAX (808) 625-6363

University of Hawaii
2800 Woodlawn Drive, Suite 280
Honolulu, HI 96822
(808) 539-3831
FAX (808) 539-3833

IDAHO

Idaho SBDC
Boise State University
1910 University Drive
Boise, ID 83725
(208) 385-1640
(208) 385-3870 (Tech consultant)
FAX (208) 385-3877

Idaho Department of Water Resources
Attn. Bioenergy Specialist
Box 83720
Boise, ID 83702-0098
(208) 327-7959

Idaho Innovation Center
2300 North Yellowstone
Idaho Falls, ID 83401
(208) 523-1026
FAX (208) 523-1049

Technical & Industrial Extension Services
Boise State University
1910 University Drive
Boise, ID 83752
(208) 385-3689
FAX (208) 385-3877

ILLINOIS

Illinois SBDC
Department of Commerce and Community Affairs
620 East Adams Street, 6th Floor
Springfield, IL 62701
(217) 524-5856
FAX (217) 524-0171

Alongi Enterprises
P.O. Box 344
Du Quoin, IL 62832
(618) 542-3613

American Electronics Assoc.
625 North Court
Palatine, IL 60067
(708) 358-2705
FAX (708) 358-3246

ARCH Development Corp.
9700 South Cass Avenue
Building 200
Argonne, IL 60439
(708) 252-5904
FAX (708) 252-2876

The Argonne National Laboratory's Study of Innovative Programs for Inventors
Environmental Systems Division
Mail Stop 362 2B
Argonne, IL 60439
(708) 972-2000

Bureau of Economic and Business Research
University of Illinois
408 David Kinley Hall
Urbana, IL 61801
(217) 333-0960
FAX (217) 333-5847

Business Technology Incubator
Bradley University
Peoria, IL 61625
(309) 677-2852
FAX (309) 677-3386

Corporate Technology Sourcing
Baxter International
P.O. Box 490
Round Lake, IL 60073
(708) 948-2000

Evanston Business & Technology Center
1840 Oak Avenue
Evanston, IL 60201
(708) 866-1817
FAX (708) 866-1808

Great Cities Coordinating Office
University of Illinois at Chicago
1737 West Polk Street, Suite 310
Chicago, IL 60612-7227
(312) 996-4995
FAX (312) 413-0238

Innovation Development Corp.
P.O. Box 1185
Calumet City, IL 60409
(708) 891-0316
FAX (708) 891-0316

Office of Technology & Commerce
Southern Illinois University
Campus Box 1108
Edwardsville, IL 62026
(618) 692-2166
FAX (618) 692-2555

Technology Commercialization Center
Illinois State University
Novey Hall 401L
Normal, IL 61761
(309) 438-2111
FAX (309) 438-8192

Technology Commercialization Office
Northern Illinois University
DeKalb, IL 60115-2874
(815) 753-1238

Technology Search Int'l., Inc.
500 East Higgins Road
Elk Grove Village, IL 60007-1437
(708) 593-2111
FAX (708) 593-2182

Technology Transfer Program
Northwestern University
633 Clark Street
Evanston, IL 60208-1111
(708) 491-3005
FAX (708) 491-3005

INDIANA

Indiana SBDC
Economic Development Council
One North Capitol, Suite 420
Indianapolis, IN 46204
(317) 264-6871
FAX (317) 264-3102

Indiana Inventors' Assoc.
5514 South Adams
Marion, IN 46953
(317) 674-2845
(317) 745-5597 (in Indianapolis)

Indiana University
Industrial Resources Liaison Program
One City Center, Suite 200
Bloomington, IN 47404
(812) 855-6294
FAX (812) 855-8270

Inventors & Entrepreneurs Society of Indiana
P.O. Box 2224
Hammond, IN 46323
(219) 989-2354
FAX (219) 989-2750

IOWA

Iowa SBDC
Iowa State University
137 Lynn Avenue
Ames, IA 50014
(515) 292-6351
FAX (515) 292-0020

Inventors, Innovators, Ideas, Inc.
304 West 2nd Street
Davenport, IA 52801
(319) 322-4499
FAX (319) 322-8241

Inventure Program
Drake University
2507 University Avenue
Des Moines, IA 50311
(515) 271-2655
FAX (515) 271-4540

KANSAS

Kansas SBDC
Wichita State University
1845 Fairmount
Wichita, KS 67260-0148
(316) 689-3193
(316) 689-3155 (Patent librarian)
FAX (316) 689-3647

Business & Technology Institute
Pittsburg State University
Pittsburg, KS 66762-7560
(316) 235-4920
FAX (316) 689-3048

Center for Research, Inc.
University of Kansas
2291 Irving Hill Road Campus
West Lawrence, KS 66045
(913) 864-3956

Innovative Technology Enterprise Corp.
112 West 6th Street, Suite 408
Topeka, KS 66603
(913) 233-9102
FAX (913) 296-1160

Kansas Assoc. of Inventors
2015 Lakin
Great Bend, KS 67530
(316) 792-1374
FAX (316) 792-3406

KENTUCKY

Kentucky SBDC
University of Kentucky
225 Business & Economics Building
Lexington, KY 40506-0034
(606) 257-7668
FAX (606) 323-1907

Bluegrass Inventors' Guild
P.O. Box 43610
Louisville, KY 40253-0610
(502) 423-9850
FAX (502) 423-1452

LOUISIANA

Louisiana SBDC
Northeast Louisiana University
700 University Avenue
Monroe, LA 71209-6435
(318) 342-5506
FAX (318) 342-5510

Business & Technology Center
Louisiana State University
South Stadium Drive
Baton Rouge, LA 70803-6100
(504) 334-5555
FAX (504) 388-3975

Louisiana Department of Economic Development
Attn. Economic Development Specialist
P.O. Box 94185
Baton Rouge, LA 70804-9185
(504) 342-5371

Southern Technology Development
109 Brownlee Avenue
Broussard, LA 70518-3021
(318) 837-4042
FAX (318) 837-5552

MAINE

Maine SBDC
University of Southern Maine
96 Falmouth Street
P.O. Box 9300
Portland, ME 04104-9300
(207) 780-4420
FAX (207) 780-4810

Center for Innovation and Entrepreneurship
University of Maine
5711 Boardman Hall
Orono, ME 04469-5711
(207) 581-1488

MARYLAND

Maryland SBDC
Department of Economic and Employment Development
217 East Redwood Street, 10th Floor
Baltimore, MD 21202
(410) 333-6995
FAX (410) 333-4460

Capital Inventors' Society
2106 Salisbury Road
Silver Springs, MD 20910
(301) 585-1885

National Institute of Standards and Technology – NIST
Building 411, Room A115
Gaithersburg, MD 20899-0001
(301) 975-5500
FAX (301) 975-3839

Technology Transfer Information Center
National Agricultural Library
10301 Baltimore Blvd.
Beltsville, MD 20705-2351
(301) 504-6875
FAX (301) 504-7098

MASSACHUSETTS

Massachusetts SBDC
University of Massachusetts – Amherst
School of Management, Room 205
Amherst, MA 01003
(413) 545-6301
FAX (413) 545-1273

Douglas Industries, Inc.
P.O. Box 581
Osterville, MA 02655
(508) 420-2002

EKMS, Inc.
100 Inman Street
Cambridge, MA 02139
(617) 864-4706
FAX (617) 864-7956

High Tech Design
26 Murray Street
West Peabody, MA 01960
(508) 535-2543

Innovation Center
Massachusetts Institute of Technology, Room 33-111
Cambridge, MA 02139
(617) 253-1000

Innovative Products Research & Services
393 Beacon Street
Lowell, MA 01850
(508) 934-0035

Inventors' Assoc. of New England
115 Abbot Street
Andover, MA 01810
(508) 474-0488

Technology Capitol Network
201 Vassar Street
Cambridge, MA 02139
(617) 253-8214
FAX (617) 258-7264

Worcester Area Inventors
65 Windsor Street
Worcester, MA 01605
(508) 757-6178

MICHIGAN

Michigan SBDC
2727 Second Avenue
Detroit, MI 48201
(313) 964-1798
FAX (313) 964-3648

Economic Development Corp.
P.O. Box 387
Traverse City, MI 49685
(616) 946-1596
FAX (616) 946-2565

Industrial Development Center
311 Houghton Street
Ontonagon, MI 49953
(906) 884-2795

InnCom
P.O. Box 507
Ypsilanti, MI 48197
(313) 963-0616
FAX (313) 963-7606

Manistee County Economic Development Office
375 River Street, Suite 205
Manistee, MI 49660
(616) 723-4325
FAX (616) 723-1488

Technology Transfer Center
Ferris State University
1020 East Maple Street
Big Rapids, MI 49307
(616) 592-3774
FAX (616) 592-1448

University of Michigan
College of Engineering
2901 Hubbard
Ann Arbor, MI 48109-2016
(313) 747-0041
FAX (313) 747-0036

MINNESOTA

Minnesota SBDC
121 Seventh Place East, Suite 500
St. Paul, MN 55101-2146
(612) 297-5770
FAX (612) 296-1290

Accessible Technologies, Inc.
494 Curfew
St. Paul, MN 55104
(612) 659-0569
FAX (612) 645-3675

The Collaborative
New Venture Research Corp.
10 South 5th Street, Suite 415
Minneapolis, MN 55402
(612) 338-3828
FAX (612) 338-1876

Excel Development Group, Inc.
1721 Mount Curve Avenue
Minneapolis, MN 55403-1017
(612) 374-3233
FAX (612) 377-0865

INNO TECH, Inc.
7007 Dakota Avenue
ChanHassen, MN 55317
(612) 937-1413
FAX (612) 934-1180

Inventors & Designers Assoc.
P.O. Box 268
Stillwater, MN 55082
(612) 430-1116

Inventors' Network
818 Dunwoody Blvd.
Minneapolis, MN 55403
(612) 933-8911

Marra Design Associates, Inc.
7007 Dakota Avenue
ChanHassen, MN 55317
(612) 937-8141
FAX (612) 934-1180

Metro ECSU Young Inventors Fair
3499 Lexington Avenue, North
St. Paul, MN 55126
(612) 490-0058
FAX (612) 490-1920

Minnesota Entrepreneurs' Club
1000 LaSelle Avenue
Minneapolis, MN 55403-2005
(612) 533-1932
FAX (612) 533-1865

Minnesota Inventors' Congress
1030 East Bridge Street
P.O. Box 71
Redwood Falls, MN 56283
(507) 637-2344
FAX (507) 637-5929

Minnesota Project Innovation, Inc.
111 Third Avenue, South, Suite 100
Minneapolis, MN 55401-2551
(612) 338-3280
FAX (612) 338-3483

Minnesota Technology, Inc.
Center for Economic Development UMD
Olcott Plaza, Suite 140
820 North 9th Street
Virginia, MN 55792
(218) 741-4241
FAX (218) 741-4249

NordicTrack
Product Planning & Development
104 Peavey Road
Chaska, MN 55318
(612) 368-2777
FAX (612) 368-2781

Society of Minnesota Inventors
20231 Basalt Street
Anoka, MN 55303
(612) 753-2766

MISSISSIPPI

Mississippi SBDC
University of Mississippi
Old Chemistry Building, Suite 216
University, MS 38677
(601) 232-5001
FAX (601) 232-5650

Bureau of Business and Economic Research
Jackson State University
1400 J.R. Lynch Street
Jackson, MS 39217
(601) 968-2121
FAX (601) 968-2007

Delta Inventors' Society
P.O. Box 257
Stoneville, MS 38776
(601) 686-4041
FAX (601) 686-4045

Society of Mississippi Inventors
P.O. Box 13004
Jackson, MS 39236-3004
(601) 982-6229
FAX (601) 982-6610

MISSOURI

Missouri SBDC
University of Missouri
300 University Place
Columbia, MO 65211
(314) 882-0344
FAX (314) 884-4297

Center for Technology
Central Missouri State University
Grinstead 80
Warrensburg, MO 64093
(816) 543-4402

Center for Technology Development & Transfer
University of Missouri
Building 1, Nagogami Terrace
Rolla, MO 65401
(314) 341-4559
FAX (314) 341-4992

EnTech Engineering, Inc.
1846 Craig Park Court
St. Louis, MO 63146
(314) 434-5255
FAX (314) 434-3270

Innovation Institute
Route 2, Box 184
Everton, MO 65646
(417) 836-6302
FAX (417) 836-6337

Mid-America Inventors
2018 Baltimore
Kansas City, MO 64108
(816) 221-2442
FAX (816) 221-3995

Mid-Missouri Inventors' Assoc.
University of Missouri – Columbia
1800 University Place
Columbia, MO 65211
(314) 882-7096
FAX (314) 882-9931

Missouri Innovation Center
5650-A South Sinclair Road
Columbia, MO 65203
(314) 446-3100
FAX (314) 443-3748

St. Louis Technology Center
P.O. Box 12405
St. Louis, MO 63132
(314) 432-4204
FAX (314) 432-1250

Washington University
1 Brookings Drive
Campus Box 1054
St. Louis, MO 63130
(314) 935-5825
FAX (314) 935-5862

MONTANA

Montana SBDC
Montana Department of Commerce
1424 Ninth Avenue
Helena, MT 59620
(406) 444-4780
FAX (406) 444-2808

Business Development Center
305 West Mercury Street
Butte, MT 59701
(406) 723-4061

Creativity, Innovation, Productivity, Inc.
RR #1, Box 37
Highwood, MT 59450
(406) 733-5031

Montana Department of Natural Resources & Conservation
Attn. Bioenergy Specialist
1520 East 6th Avenue
P.O. Box 202301
Helena, MT 59620-2301
(406) 444-6697
FAX (406) 444-6721

Montana Entrepreneurship Center
Montana State University
Reid Hall
Bozeman, MT 59717
(406) 994-2024
FAX (406) 994-4152

Montana Entrepreneurship Center
University of Montana
McGill Hall, Suite 204
Missoula, MT 59812
(406) 243-4009
FAX (406) 243-4030

Montana Inventors' Assoc.
5350 Love Lane
Bozeman, MT 59715
(406) 586-1541
FAX (406) 585-9028

Montana Science & Technology Alliance
46 North Last Chance Gulch, Suite 2B
Helena, MT 59620
(406) 449-2778
FAX (406) 442-0788

Montana Tradeport Authority
2722 3rd Avenue, North, Suite 300W
Billings, MT 59101-1931
(406) 256-6871
FAX (406) 256-6877

Research & Development Institute
Montana State University
1711 West College
Bozeman, MT 59715
(406) 587-4479
FAX (406) 587-4480

Yellowstone Inventors' Assoc.
3 Carrie Lynn
Billings, MT 59102
(406) 259-9110

NEBRASKA

Nebraska Business Development Center
University of Nebraska at Omaha
1313 Farnam, Suite 132
Omaha, NE 68182
(402) 554-2521
FAX (402) 554-3747

The Development Council
1007 Second Avenue
P.O. Box 607
Kearney, NE 68848
(308) 237-9346
FAX (308) 237-3103

University of Nebraska – Lincoln Engineering Extension
W191 Nebraska Hall
Lincoln, NE 68588-0535
(402) 472-5600
FAX (402) 472-2410

NEVADA

Nevada SBDC
University of Nevada – Reno
College of Business Administration, Room 411
Reno, NV 89557-0100
(702) 784-1717
FAX (702) 784-4337

Concept Support and Development Corp.
121 Woodland Avenue, Suite 100
Reno, NV 89523
(702) 746-0700

Institute for Business & Industry
4001 South Virginia Street
Reno, NV 89502
(702) 829-9000
FAX (702) 829-9009

Nevada Inventors' Assoc.
P.O. Box 9905
Reno, NV 89507-0905
(702) 322-9636
(702) 877-1161 (in Carson City)

South Nevada Certified Development Co.
2770 South Maryland Parkway, Suite 212
Las Vegas, NV 89109
(702) 732-3998
FAX (702) 732-2705

NEW HAMPSHIRE

New Hampshire SBDC
University of New Hampshire
108 McConnell Hall
Durham, NH 03824
(603) 862-2200
FAX (603) 862-4876

I.D.E.A.
Star Route, Box 98
Meridan, NH 03770
(603) 469-3304
FAX (603) 469-3305

PROMARK Consulting Services
P.O. Box 5249
Hanover, NH 03755
(603) 643-3043

TechWorks
Attn. License Consultant
15 Kancamagus Estates
P.O. Box 337
Conway, NH 03818-0337
(603) 447-6331

NEW JERSEY

New Jersey SBDC
Rutgers University
School of Business
180 University Avenue
Newark, NJ 07102
(201) 648-5950
(201) 648-1597 (Technology help desk)
FAX (201) 648-1110

National Society of Inventors
P.O. Box 434
Cranford, NJ 07016
(201) 994-9282

NEW MEXICO

New Mexico SBDC
Santa Fe Community College
P.O. Box 4187
Santa Fe, NM 87502-4187
(505) 438-1362
FAX (505) 438-1237

Economic Development Corp.
P.O. Box 715
Los Alamos, NM 87544
(505) 662-0001
FAX (505) 662-0099

New Mexico State University
Research & Economic Development
Box 30001, Dept 3
Las Cruces, NM 88003
(505) 646-2022
FAX (505) 646-6530

New Mexico Tech
Research & Economic Development
College Avenue
Socorro, NM 87801
(505) 835-5646
FAX (505) 835-5649

Technical Applications Center
University of New Mexico
Albuquerque, NM 87131
(505) 277-0111
FAX (505) 277-6019

Technology Venture Corp.
4919 Marble, NE
Albuquerque, NM 87110
(505) 246-2882
FAX (505) 246-2891

University of New Mexico
Anderson School of Management
Albuquerque, NM 87131-1221
(505) 277-6471
FAX (505) 277-7108

NEW YORK

New York State SBDC
State University of New York
SUNY Central Plaza, S-523
Albany, NY 12246
(518) 443-5398
FAX (518) 465-4992

Aztech, Inc.
1576 Sweet Home Road
Amherst, NY 14228
(716) 636-3028
FAX (916) 636-3630

InfoEd
453 New Karner Road
Albany, NY 12205
(518) 464-0691
FAX (518) 464-0695

Information Services and Research
P.O. Box 95
Syracuse, NY 13210
(315) 476-7359

Inventor's Helper
P.O. Box 68
Dix Hills, NY 11746
(800) 633-9727
FAX (800) 633-3292

Inventors' Workshop Internat'l. Education Fdtn. – IWIEF
Syracuse Chapter
205 South Central Avenue
Minoa, NY 13116
(315) 656-9210

New York Society of Professional Inventors
116 Steuart Avenue
Amityville, NY 11701
(516) 598-3228
FAX (516) 598-3241

New York Society of Professional Inventors
State University of New York
College of Technology
Lupton Hall
Farmingdale, NY 11735
(516) 420-2397

Patent Research Services
P.O. Box 68
Dix Hills, NY 11746
(800) 835-0880
FAX (800) 633-3292

Smith Engineering
114-56 142nd Street
Jamaica, NY 11436
(718) 529-3434

Technical Information Assoc.
New York State Energy Authority
2 Empire State Plaza, Suite 1901
Albany, NY 12223-1253
(518) 465-6251
FAX (518) 432-9474

Technology Business Advisory Group
100 Kinloch Commons
Manlius, NY 13104-2484
(315) 682-8502
FAX (315) 682-8508

Toy Manufacturers of America, Inc.
Room 740
200 Fifth Avenue
New York, NY 10010
(212) 675-1141
FAX (212) 633-1929

Western New York Technical Development Center
200 Harrison Street
Jamestown, NY 14701
(716) 661-3336
FAX (716) 483-4470

NORTH CAROLINA

North Carolina SBDC
University of North Carolina
4509 Creedmoor Road, Suite 201
Raleigh, NC 27612
(919) 571-4154
FAX (919) 571-4161

North Carolina Technological Development Authority, Inc.
2 Davis Drive
P.O. Box 13169
Research Triangle Park, NC 27709
(919) 990-8558
FAX (919) 990-8561

Small Business Technical Development Center
34 Wall Street, Room 707
Asheville, NC 28801
(704) 285-0021

Edward White, Consultant
907 Linden Road
Chapel Hill, NC 27514-7742
(919) 929-7283
FAX (919) 933-9233

NORTH DAKOTA

North Dakota SBDC
University of North Dakota
118 Gamble Hall, Box 7308
Grand Forks, ND 58202
(701) 777-3700
FAX (701) 777-5099

Center for Innovation and Business Development
University of North Dakota
University Station, Box 8372
Grand Forks, ND 58202
(701) 777-3132
FAX (701) 777-2339

Garrison Area Improvement Assoc.
P.O. Box 445
Garrison, ND 58540
(701) 463-2631
FAX (701) 463-7487

Technology Transfer, Inc.
1833 East Bismarck Expressway
Bismarck, ND 58504
(701) 221-5346
FAX (701) 221-5320

OHIO

Ohio SBDC
77 South High Street
P.O. Box 1001
Columbus, OH 43266-0101
(614) 466-2711
FAX (614) 466-0829

Akron/Youngstown Inventors
1225 West Market Street
Akron, OH 44313
(216) 864-5550
FAX (216) 867-7986

Center for Economic Education
University of Akron
213 Crouse Hall
Akron, OH 44325-4210
(216) 972-7762
FAX (216) 972-6990

Edison Industrial Systems Center
1700 North Westwood Avenue,
Suite 2286
Toledo, OH 43607-1207
(419) 531-8610
FAX (419) 531-8465

Hopewell Cooperation, Inc.
73 Maplewood Drive
Athens, OH 45701-1910
(614) 594-5200
FAX (614) 594-4004

Invention Connection of Cleveland
P.O. Box 360804
Cleveland, OH 44136
(216) 226-9681

Invention Engineering, Inc.
27 Aberdeen Avenue
Dayton, OH 45419-3101
(513) 294-7447
FAX (513) 294-7448

Inventors' Council of Dayton
P.O. Box 630
Dayton, OH 45459-0630
(513) 439-4497
FAX (513) 439-1704

Inventors' Network, Inc.
1275 Kinnear Road
Columbus, OH 43219
(614) 291-7900

Inventor's Society at Northwest, Ohio
617 Croghan Street
Fremont, OH 43420
(419) 332-2221
FAX (419) 334-6164

Inventure Place – Home of Nat'l Inventors Hall of Fame
80 West Bowery, Suite 201
Akron, OH 44308
(216) 762-4463
FAX (216) 762-6313

Kessler Corp.
1247 Napoleon Street
Fremont, OH 43420
(800) 537-1133
FAX (419) 334-5068

National Business Incubation Assoc.
20 East Circle Drive, Suite 190
Athens, OH 45701
(614) 593-4331
FAX (614) 593-1996

Ohio Technology Transfer Center
1080 Carmack Road
Bevis Hall, Room 216
Columbus, OH 43210
(614) 292-5485
FAX (614) 292-1893

Yankee Ingenuity Programs
623 Grant Street
Kent, OH 44240
(216) 673-1875
FAX (216) 678-5743

Warren Inventors' Assoc.
3220 Eldora Drive
Youngstown, OH 44511
(216) 792-4880

OKLAHOMA

Oklahoma SBDC
Southeastern Oklahoma State University
P.O. Box 2584, Station A
Durant, OK 74701
(405) 924-0277
FAX (405) 920-7471

Invention Development Society
8230 SW 8th Street
Oklahoma City, OK 73128
(405) 787-0145
FAX (405) 789-8198

Inventors' Resource and Technology Center
100 South University Avenue,
Room 106
Enid, OK 73701
(405) 242-7989
FAX (405) 237-2304

New Technology Ventures, Inc.
7649 SW 34th Street
Oklahoma City, OK 73179
(405) 745-7800
FAX (405) 745-2276

Oklahoma Inventors' Congress
P.O. Box 27850
Tulsa, OK 74149-0850
(918) 245-6465
FAX (918) 245-2947

Oklahoma Student Inventors' Exposition
8230 SW 8th Street
Oklahoma City, OK 73128
(405) 787-0145

O.T. Autry Area Vocational Technical School
1201 West Willow
Enid, OK 73703
(405) 242-2750
FAX (405) 233-8262

Rural Enterprises, Inc.
P.O. Box 1335
Durant, OK 74701
(405) 924-5094
FAX (405) 920-2745

OREGON

Oregon SBDC
Lane Community College
44 West Broadway, Suite 501
Eugene, OR 97401-3201
(541) 726-2250
FAX (541) 345-6006

Business Information Center
Public Service Building, Suite 151
255 Capitol Street, NE
Salem, OR 97310-1327
(503) 986-2222

Phyllis Lohse, Business Consultant
2123 SW Greene
West Linn, OR 97068-4107
(503) 655-3410
FAX (503) 657-5138

MarketLink Strategies
P.O. Box 42182
Portland, OR 97242
(503) 232-1514
FAX (503) 234-3731

Oregon Resource and Technology Development Fund – ORTDF
4370 NE Halsey, Suite 233
Portland, OR 97213-1566
(503) 282-4462
FAX (503) 282-2976

Theodore Texas & Associates
P.O. Box 4633
Portland, OR 97208
(503) 244-6447
FAX (503) 246-4859

Unitor Corp.
P.O. Box 309
Silverton, OR 97381
(503) 873-7746
FAX (503) 873-7746

Venture Solutions, Ltd.
4500 SW Kruseway, Suite 220
Lake Oswego, OR 97035
(503) 635-4647

PENNSYLVANIA

Pennsylvania SBDC
University of Pennsylvania
444 Vance Hall, 3733 Spruce Street
Philadelphia, PA 19104-6374
(215) 898-1219
FAX (215) 573-2135

American Society of Inventors
P.O. Box 58426
Philadelphia, PA 19102
(215) 546-6601

Domestic & International Tech, Ltd.
115 West Avenue
Jenkintown, PA 19046
(215) 885-7670
FAX (215) 884-1385

Inventors' Assistance
Lehigh University
621 Taylor Street
Bethlehem, PA 18015
(215) 758-3446
FAX (215) 758-4499

Northwestern Inventors' Council
Gannon University
Erie, PA 16541
(814) 871-7619
FAX (814) 455-2631

Product Development Center
Bucknell University
126 Dana Engineering Building
Lewisburg, PA 17837
(717) 524-1249
FAX (717) 524-1768

Techni-Research Assoc., Inc.
P.O. Box T
Willow Grove, PA 19090-0922
(215) 657-1753
FAX (215) 576-7924

University City Science Center
3624 Market Street
Philadelphia, PA 19104
(215) 387-2255
FAX (215) 382-0056

RHODE ISLAND

Rhode Island SBDC
Bryant College
1150 Douglas Pike
Smithfield, RI 02917
(401) 232-6111
FAX (401) 232-6416

Rhode Island Partnership for Science & Technology
7 Jackson Walkway
Providence, RI 02903
(401) 277-2601
FAX (401) 277-2102

Rhode Island Solar Energy Assoc.
42 Tremont Street
Cranston, RI 02920-2543
(401) 942-6691

SOUTH CAROLINA

The Frank L. Roddy SBDC
University of South Carolina
College of Business Administration
Columbia, SC 29201-9980
(803) 777-4907
FAX (803) 777-4403

Battelle Liaison
Clemson University
300 Brackett Hall
Clemson, SC 29634-5705
(803) 656-1296
FAX (803) 656-0202

Carolina Inventors' Council
2960 Dacusville Highway
Easley, SC 29640
(803) 859-0066

Economic Enterprise Institute
University of South Carolina – Aiken
171 University Parkway
Aiken, SC 29801
(803) 648-6851
FAX (803) 641-3445

Enterprise Development, Inc. of South Carolina
P.O. Box 1149
Columbia, SC 29202
(803) 252-8806
FAX (803) 252-0053

Private Investor Network
University of South Carolina
171 University Parkway
Aiken, SC 29801
(803) 648-6851
FAX (803) 641-3362

Southeast Manufacturing Tech Center
1201 Main Street, Suite 2010
P.O. Box 1149
Columbia, SC 29202
(803) 252-6976
FAX (803) 252-0056

SOUTH DAKOTA

South Dakota SBDC
University of South Dakota
414 East Clark Street
Vermillion, SD 57069
(605) 677-5279
FAX (605) 677-5277

South Dakota Public Utility Commission
State Capitol Building
500 East Capital
Pierre, SD 57501
(605) 773-3201
FAX (605) 773-3809

South Dakota State University
College of Engineering
CEH 201 Box 2219
Brookings, SD 57007-0096
(605) 688-4161
FAX (605) 688-5878

TENNESSEE

Tennessee SBDC
Memphis State University
Building 1, South Campus
Memphis, TN 38152
(901) 678-2500
FAX (901) 678-4072

Office of Technology Transfer
Martin Marietta Energy Systems, Inc.
P.O. Box 2009
Oak Ridge, TN 37831-8242
(615) 576-0378
FAX (615) 574-9241

Tennessee Inventors' Assoc.
P.O. Box 11225
Knoxville, TN 37939
(615) 483-0151
FAX (615) 974-5492

University of Tennessee Research Corp.
415 Communication Building
Knoxville, TN 37996-0344
(615) 974-1882
FAX (615) 974-2803

TEXAS

Texas SBDC
University of Houston
Product Development Center
1100 Louisiana, Suite 500
Houston, TX 77002
(713) 752-8440
FAX (713) 756-1500

Amarillo Inventors' Assoc.
P.O. Box 15023
Amarillo, TX 79105
(806) 376-8726
FAX (806) 376-7753

Austin Technology Incubator
8920 Business Park Drive
Austin, TX 78759
(512) 794-9994

Best Concept P.D. Co.
1212 Collinwood West Drive
Austin, TX 78753
(512) 834-7886

The Capital Network
8920 Business Park Drive, Suite 275
Austin, TX 78759
(512) 794-9398
FAX (512) 794-0448

Center for Enterprise and Entrepreneurship
Baylor University
Hankamer School of Business,
Suite 308
P.O. Box 98011
Waco, TX 76798
(817) 755-2265
FAX (817) 755-2271

Da Vinci Design
15207 McConn
Webster, TX 77598
(713) 280-9473
FAX (713) 280-9152

Entrepreneurs Online
10550 Richmond Avenue,
Suite 200
Houston, TX 77042
(713) 784-8822
FAX (713) 735-2900

Houston Inventors' Assoc.
204 Yacht Club Lane
Seabrook, TX 77586
(713) 326-1795

Information Insights
1418 Fairwood Road
Austin, TX 78722
(512) 451-8871
FAX (512) 451-1885

Inventors' Information Systems
P.O. Box 927
Abilene, TX 79604
(915) 698-3318
FAX (915) 673-4855

Johnson Technology Commercialization Center
National Aeronautics & Space Administration
2200 Space Park Drive, Suite 200
Houston, TX 77058
(713) 335-1250
FAX (713) 333-9285

Network of American Inventors and Entrepreneurs
11371 Walters Road
Houston, TX 77067
(713) 537-8277

Technology Transfer Center
Bill J. Priest Institute for Economic Development
1402 Corinth
Dallas, TX 75215
(214) 565-5852
FAX (214) 565-5881

Texas Inventors' Assoc.
4000 Rock Creek Drive, Suite 100
Dallas, TX 75204
(817) 265-1540

Toy & Game Inventors of America
5813 McCart Avenue
Ft. Worth, TX 76133
(817) 292-9021
FAX (817) 346-8697

Ultimate Concepts, Inc.
P.O. Box 740304
Houston, TX 77274
(713) 873-6338
FAX (713) 778-9092

U.S. Department of Energy
Dallas Support Office
1420 West Mockingbird Lane,
Suite 400
Dallas, TX 75247
(214) 767-7245
FAX (214) 767-7231

Venture Assistance
5807 South Braeswood Blvd.
Houston, TX 77096
(713) 729-1129

UTAH

Utah SBDC
University of Utah
102 West 500 South, Suite 315
Salt Lake City, UT 84101
(801) 581-7905
FAX (801) 581-7814

Business Creation
324 South State Street, Suite 500
Salt Lake City, UT 84114-7380
(801) 538-8770
FAX (801) 538-8773

Center for Entrepreneurship Training
P.O. Box 30808
Salt Lake City, UT 84130-8080
(801) 967-4558
FAX (801) 967-4017

Intermountain Society of Inventors and Designers
9888 Darin Drive
Sandy, UT 84070
(801) 571-2617

Project Outreach
P.O. Box 1106
Price, UT 84501
(801) 637-5444
FAX (801) 637-5448

Science, Technology & Innovation State Office
P.O. Box 11
West Jordan, UT 84084
(801) 569-2973

Technology Assistance Center
Weber State University
Ogden, UT 84408-1801
(801) 626-6309
FAX (801) 626-6987

Utah Innovation Center
University of Utah
417 Wakara Way
Salt Lake City, UT 84112
(801) 581-7200
FAX (801) 581-7880

VERMONT

Vermont SBDC
Vermont Technical College
P.O. Box 422
Randolph, VT 05060
(802) 728-9101
FAX (802) 728-3026

The Catalyst Group
P.O. Box 1200
Brattleboro, VT 05302-1200
(802) 254-3645
FAX (802) 254-3645

Vermont Agency of Development & Commercial Affairs
Montpelier, VT 05609
(802) 828-3221
FAX (802) 828-3258

VIRGINIA

Virginia SBDC
901 East Byrd Street, Suite 1800
Richmond, VA 23219
(804) 371-8253
FAX (804) 225-3384

Keller Patent Consulting
P.O. Box 10051
Alexandria, VA 22310
(703) 960-1037
FAX (703) 960-9530

National Technology Transfer Center
Wheeling Jesuit College
2121 Eisenhower Avenue, Suite 400
Alexandria, VA 22314
(703) 518-8800
FAX (703) 518-8986

NJ Commission on Science & Technology
4156 Elizabeth Lane
Annadale, VA 22003
(703) 425-4825
FAX (703) 425-6736

Renewable Energy Clearinghouse
P.O. Box 3048
Merrifield, VA 22110
(800) 523-2929

Technology Commercialization Center for Innovative Technology
CIT Building, Suite 600
2214 Rock Hill Road
Herndon, VA 22070
(703) 689-3000
FAX (703) 689-3041

Virginia Tech Graduate Center
2990 Telestar Court
Falls Church, VA 22042
(703) 698-6016
FAX (703) 698-6062

WASHINGTON

Washington SBDC
Washington State University
Kruegel Hall, Room 135
Pullman, WA 99164-4727
(509) 335-1576
FAX (509) 335-0949

The Business Consortium, Inc.
P.O. Box 599
Wilbur, WA 99185
(509) 647-2000
FAX (509) 647-2001

Critical Data, Inc.
906 South Cowley
Spokane, WA 99202
(509) 838-2917
FAX (509) 838-4989

Federal Laboratory Consortium
Management Support Office
P.O. Box 545
Sequim, WA 98382-0545
(206) 683-1005
FAX (206) 683-6654

Innovation Assessment Center
Washington State University
180 Nickerson Street, Suite 207
Seattle, WA 98109
(206) 464-5450
FAX (206) 464-6357

Northwest Regional Technology Transfer Center
National Aeronautics & Space Administration
12318 NE 100th Place
Kirkland, WA 98033
(206) 827-5136
FAX (206) 827-5430

Office of Technology Transfer
University of Washington
1107 NE 45th Street, Suite 200
Seattle, WA 98105
(206) 543-3970
FAX (206) 685-4767

Seattle University
Albers School of Business & Economics
Broadway and Madison
Seattle, WA 98122-4460
(206) 296-5702
FAX (206) 296-5795

Technology Targeting, Inc.
7454 South 118th Place
Seattle, WA 98178-3039
(206) 227-8088
FAX (206) 227-8068

Tri-Cities Enterprise Assoc.
2000 Logston Blvd.
Richland, WA 99352
(509) 375-3268
FAX (509) 375-4838

Washington State University
Attn. Marketing Department
100 Sprout Road
Richland, WA 99352-1643
(509) 375-9207
FAX (509) 375-5337

Western Investment Network
Burton Station, P.O. Box 13310
Vashon Island, WA 98013
(206) 441-3123
FAX (206) 463-6386

WEST VIRGINIA

West Virginia Small Business Development Center
950 Kanawha Blvd., East
Charleston, WV 25301
(304) 558-2960
FAX (304) 558-0127

WISCONSIN

Wisconsin SBDC
University of Wisconsin
432 North Lake Street, Room 423
Madison, WI 53706
(608) 263-7794
FAX (608) 262-3878

Wisconsin Department of Development
P.O. Box 7970
Madison, WI 53707
(608) 267-9383
FAX (608) 267-2829

Wisconsin Innovation Service Center
University of Wisconsin
402 McCutchan Hall
Whitewater, WI 52190
(414) 472-1365
FAX (414) 472-1600

WYOMING

Wyoming SBDC Network
P.O. Box 3275
Laramie, WY 82071-3275
(307) 766-3505
FAX (307) 766-3406

West Inventors' Council
109 Engineering Research
P.O. Box 6101
Morgantown, WY 26506-6101
(304) 293-3612
FAX (304) 293-3472

FOREIGN COUNTRIES

AMERICAN SAMOA

Economic Development Planning Office
American Samoa Government
Pago Pago, American Samoa, 96799
American Samoa
(684) 633-5155
FAX (684) 633-4195

CANADA

Canadian Center for Industry, Innovation, Evaluation & Technology Transfer
75 Port Royal East, Suite 600
Montreal, Quebec H3L 3T1
(514) 383-7712
FAX (514) 383-7040

Canadian Industrial Innovation Center
156 Columbia Street, West
Waterloo, Ontario N2L 3L3
(519) 885-5870
FAX (519) 885-5729

Canadian Young Inventors' Fair Society
Box 12151
1220-808 Nelson Street
Vancouver, BC V6Z 2H2
(604) 689-3626
FAX (604) 684-4589

Copyrights, Inventions & Patents Assoc. of Canada
1518 Dome Tower
333-7 Avenue, SW
Calgary, Alberta T2P 2Z1
(403) 265-3011
FAX (403) 266-4091

Guerin Science & Technology
1060 Walden Circle, Unit 11
Mississauga, Ontario L5J 4J9
(905) 855-5357

Intellectual Property Analyst Concept Licensing Corp.
1518 Dome Tower
333-7 Avenue, SW
Calgary, Alberta T2P 2Z1
(403) 265-3011
FAX (403) 266-4091

Inventors' Alliance of Canada
47 Kenneth Avenue
Toronto, Ontario M6P 1J1
(416) 762-3453
FAX (416) 762-3301

Inventors' Society of Nova Scotia
1046 Barrington Street, Suite 106
Halifax, Nova Scotia B3H 2R1
(902) 421-1250
FAX (902) 429-9983

Nova Scotia Department of Economic Development
1800 Argyle
P.O. Box 519
Halifax, Nova Scotia B3J 2R7
(902) 424-7382
FAX (902) 424-5739

Technical Transfer Office
University/Industry Liaison
Simon Fraser University
Burnby, BC V5A 1S6
(604) 291-5844
FAX (604) 291-3477

The University of Western Ontario
London, Ontario N6A 5B8
(519) 661-2161
FAX (519) 661-3907

Women Inventors' Project
1 Greensboro Drive, Suite 302
Etobicoke, Ontario M9W1C8
(416) 243-0668
FAX (416) 243-0688

GUAM

Solarville
P.O. Box 1167
Agana, Guam 96910
(671) 472-8131
FAX (671) 472-8131

PUERTO RICO

Puerto Rico Products Assoc.
P.O. Box 363631
San Juan, Puerto Rico 00936-3631
(809) 753-8484
FAX (809) 753-0855

Puerto Rico: SBDC
Box 5253, College Station
Mayaguez, Puerto Rico 00681
(809) 834-5556
FAX (809) 832-5550

ROMANIA

National Inventics Institute of Jassy
P.O. Box 727
Iasi-3, Romania RO-6600
(40) 98-146577
FAX (40) 98-147923

SWITZERLAND

World Intellectual Property Organization
34 Chemin des Colombettes
1211 Geneva 20
Switzerland
(022) 730-9111
FAX (022) 733-5428

B

Patent Depository Libraries

This appendix features a state-by-state listing of patent depository libraries. A patent depository library is an extension of the U.S. Patent and Trademark Science Library in Arlington, Virginia, and houses copies of patents dating back to 1790 for research.

If possible, use the resources available at the U.S. Patent and Trademark Office Science Library. It is considered the nation's main patent library.

U.S. Patent and Trademark Office Science Library
Crystal Plaza 34
2021 Jefferson Davis Highway
Arlington, VA 22202
(703) 305-8800
FAX (703) 305-8825

ALABAMA

Auburn University Library
Auburn University
Auburn, AL 36849
(205) 826-4500

Birmingham Public Library
21 Park Place
Birmingham, AL 35203
(205) 226-3680

ALASKA

Anchorage Municipal Libraries
(907) 264-4481

ARIZONA

Arizona State University Library
Tempe, AZ 85287
(602) 965-7609

ARKANSAS

Arkansas State Library
One Capitol Mall
Little Rock, AR 72201
(501) 371-2090

CALIFORNIA

California State Library
Library Courts Building
Sacramento, CA 95809
(916) 322-4572

Los Angeles Public Library
630 West Fifth Street
Los Angeles, CA 90071
(213) 612-3273

San Diego Public Library
202 C Street
San Diego, CA 92101
(619) 236-5813

Sunnyvale Public Library
Patent Information Clearinghouse
665 West Olive Avenue
Sunnyvale, CA 94086
(408) 730-7290

University of California General Library
P.O. Box 19557
Irvine, CA 92713
(714) 865-7234

COLORADO

Denver Public Library
3840 York Street
Denver, CO 80205
(303) 571-2122

CONNECTICUT

Connecticut State Library
231 Capitol Avenue
Hartford, CT 06106
(203) 786-5000

DELAWARE

University of Delaware Library
Newark, DE 19711
(302) 451-2965

FLORIDA

Broward County Main Library
100 South Andrews Avenue
Fort Lauderdale, FL 33301
(305) 357-7444

Miami-Dade Public Library
101 West Flagler Street
Miami, FL 33130
(305) 375-2665

GEORGIA

Price Gilbert Memorial Library
Georgia Institute of Technology
225 North Avenue, NW
Atlanta, GA 30332
(404) 894-4508

IDAHO

University of Idaho Library
Moscow, ID 83843
(208) 885-6235

ILLINOIS

Chicago Public Library
400 North Franklin
Chicago, IL 60602
(312) 269-2865

Illinois State Library
Centennial Building
Springfield, IL 62756
(217) 782-5430

INDIANA

Indianapolis Public Library
40 East St. Clair Street
Indianapolis, IN 46206
(317) 269-1741

LOUISIANA

Troy H. Middleton Library
Louisiana State University
Baton Rouge, LA 70803
(504) 388-2570

MARYLAND

University of Maryland Library
University of Maryland
College Park, MD 20742
(301) 454-3037

MASSACHUSETTS

Boston Public Library
Copley Square
Boston, MA 02117
(617) 536-5400

University of Massachusetts
Amherst, MA 01003
(413) 545-1370

MICHIGAN

Detroit Public Library
5201 Woodward Avenue
Detroit, MI 48202
(313) 833-1450

Hatcher Library – South
University of Michigan
818 Harlan
Ann Arbor, MI 48109
(313) 764-7494

MINNESOTA

Minneapolis Public Library
300 Nicollet Mall
Minneapolis, MN 55401
(612) 372-6570

MISSOURI

Linda Hall Library
5109 Cherry Street
Kansas City, MO 64110
(816) 363-4600

St. Louis Public Library
1301 Olive Street
St. Louis, MO 63103
(314) 241-2288

MONTANA

Montana College of Mineral Science and Technology Library
Butte, MT 59701
(406) 496-4284

NEBRASKA

University of Nebraska – Lincoln Library
Lincoln, NE 68588
(402) 472-3411

NEVADA

University of Nevada Library – Reno
Reno, NV 89557
(702) 784-6579

NEW HAMPSHIRE

University of New Hampshire Library
Durham, NH 03824
(603) 862-1777

NEW JERSEY

Newark Public Library
5 Washington Street
Newark, NJ 07101
(201) 733-7815

NEW MEXICO

General Library
University of New Mexico
Albuquerque, NM 87131
(505) 277-5441

NEW YORK

Buffalo and Erie County Public Library
Lafayette Square
Buffalo, NY 14203
(716) 856-7525

New York State Library
Cultural Education Center
Albany, NY 12230
(518) 474-7040

The New York Public Library
521 West 43rd Street
New York, NY 10036
(212) 714-8529
(212) 930-0917 (Patent librarian)

NORTH CAROLINA

The D.H. Hill Library
North Carolina State University
Raleigh, NC 27650
(919) 737-3280

OHIO

Cleveland Public Library
325 Superior Avenue
Cleveland, OH 44114
(216) 623-2870

Ohio State University Library
1858 Neil Avenue Mall
Columbus, OH 43210
(614) 422-6286

Public Library of Cincinnati
800 Vine Street
Cincinnati, OH 45202
(513) 369-6936

Toledo Public Library
325 Michigan Street
Toledo, OH 43624
(419) 255-7055

OKLAHOMA

Oklahoma State University Library
Stillwater, OK 74078
(405) 624-6546

OREGON

Patent & Trademark Depository
State Library Building
Salem, OR 97310
(503) 378-4239

Portland State University Library
934 SW Harrison
Portland, OR 97207
(503) 378-4239

PENNSYLVANIA

Carnegie Library of Pittsburgh
4400 Forbes Avenue
Pittsburgh, PA 15217
(412) 622-3138

Pattee Library
Pennsylvania State University
University Park, PA 16802
(814) 865-4861

State Library of Pennsylvania
Walnut Street and Commonwealth Avenue
Harrisburg, PA 17105
(215) 686-5330

RHODE ISLAND

Providence Public Library
150 Empire Street
Providence, RI 02903
(401) 521-8726

SOUTH CAROLINA

Medical University of South Carolina
171 Ashley Avenue
Charleston, SC 29425
(803) 792-2371

TENNESSEE

Memphis Public Library
1850 Peabody Avenue
Memphis, TN 38104
(901) 725-8876

Vanderbilt University Library
Nashville, TN 37203
(615) 322-2775

TEXAS

Dallas Public Library
1515 Young Street
Dallas, TX 75201
(214) 749-4176

The Fondren Library
Rice University
Houston, TX 77251-1892
(713) 527-8101

General Libraries
University of Texas at Austin
Austin, TX 78712
(512) 471-1610

Sterling C. Evans Library
Texas A & M University
College Station, TX 77843-5000
(409) 845-2551

UTAH

Marriott Library
University of Utah
Salt Lake City, UT 84112
(801) 581-8394

VIRGINIA

Virginia Commonwealth University Library
901 Park Avenue
Richmond, VA 23228
(804) 257-1104

WASHINGTON

Suzzallo Library
University of Washington
Seattle, WA 98195
(206) 543-0740

WISCONSIN

Kurt F. Wendt Engineering Library
University of Wisconsin
215 North Randall Avenue
Madison, WI 53706
(608) 262-6845

Milwaukee Public Library
814 West Wisconsin Avenue
Milwaukee, WI 53233
(414) 278-3247

WYOMING

Wyoming State Library
2301 Capital Avenue
Cheyenne, WY 82002
(307) 777-7281

Notes

C

Trade Shows

According to the Trade Show Bureau, nearly 85 percent of all trade show attendants have buying power, making trade shows a powerful selling strategy. Each month across the country, numerous trade shows take place, bringing together thousands of inventors, businesses, and buyers. This appendix lists only a few trade shows by the month in which they occur. Additionally, many of these listings are trade show promoters, who will have information on a number of different shows throughout the year.

For the most current information on trade shows, you can refer to your local library's business reference desk. For further information on setting up exhibits, consider obtaining a copy of these useful and informative publications listed below.

Great Show Exhibits
Designers and Producers Association
521 Fifth Avenue
New York, NY 10017

Discusses designs of trade show exhibits.

Trade Shows and Exhibits
Association of National Advertisers
115 East 4th Street
New York, NY 10017

Provides helpful information on how to prepare for trade shows.

To locate trade associations, go to the library and request a copy of one or all of the below directories. They are excellent research sources for learning about new trade associations (and shows) in your industry.

- *Directory of European Associations*
- *Encyclopedia of Associations*
- *National Trade and Professional Association Directory*

JANUARY SHOWS

Agriculture Fair
Route # 1, Box 1610
Litchfield, ME 04350
(207) 268-4631
FAX (207) 268-2032

Allied Social Science Assoc.
2014 Broadway, Suite 305
Nashville, TN 37203
(615) 322-2595
FAX (615) 343-7590

FEBRUARY SHOWS

American Marketing Assoc.
250 South Wacker Drive, Suite 200
Chicago, IL 60606
(312) 648-0536
FAX (312) 648-9713

Protech Conference
12713 Franklin Farm Road
Herndon, VA 22071
(703) 787-0000

MARCH SHOWS

American Business Women Assoc.
9100 Ward Parkway
P.O. Box 8728
Kansas City, MO 64114
(816) 361-6621
FAX (816) 361-4991

New England Products Trade Show
P.O. Box 9300
Portland, ME 04104
(207) 780-4420
FAX (207) 780-4810

APRIL SHOWS

Business Opportunity Fair
36 South Wabash, Suite 725
Chicago, IL 60603
(312) 263-0105

Business to Business Expo
1445 Market Street
Denver, CO 80202
(303) 620-8026
FAX (303) 534-3200

Industrial Show
20 West Aylesbury Road
Timonium, MD 21093
(800) 638-6396

MAY SHOWS

Affiliated Agencies Assoc.
530 Bercut Drive, Suite G
Sacramento, CA 95814
(916) 648-6536

Technology Conference
1575 I Street, NW
Washington, DC 20005-1168
(202) 371-0940
FAX (202) 371-8315

Business Show
1415 Queen Anne Road, Suite 201
Teaneck, NJ 07666
(201) 837-8200
FAX (201) 837 9770

JUNE SHOWS

American Assoc. of Exporters/Importers
11 West 42nd Street, 30th Floor
New York, NY 10036
(212) 944-2230
FAX (212) 463-4569

Direct Selling Assoc.
1666 K Street, NW, Suite 1010
Washington, DC 20006
(212) 293-5760
FAX (202) 463-4569

JULY SHOWS

American Agricultural Assoc.
1110 Buckeye Avenue
Ames, IA 50010
(515) 233-3509

AUGUST SHOWS

Invention Convention
P.O. Box 93669
Los Angeles, CA 90093-6690
(213) 460-4408
FAX (213) 962-8588

Marketing Professionals
99 Canal Central Plaza, Suite 250
Alexandria, VA 22314-1588
(703) 549-6117
FAX (703) 549-2498

SEPTEMBER SHOWS

Lincoln Products Show
1613 Faram Street, Suite 666
Omaha, NE 68102-2142
(402) 346-8003
FAX (402) 346-5412

Maine Industrial Show
352 Trapelo Road
Belmont, MA 02178-1891
(617) 489-2302
FAX (617) 489-5534

National Merchandise Show
One Penn Plaza
New York, NY 10119-0004
(212) 615-2672
FAX (212) 768-3481

OCTOBER SHOWS

International World Conference
1342 Colonial Blvd., Suite 25
Ft. Myers, FL 33907-1007
(813) 275-7887
FAX (813) 275-0794

Biotechnology Fair
103 Carnegie Center
Princeton, NJ 68540
(606) 987-1202

Industrial Expo
325 Essjay Road, Suite 100
Williamsville, NY 14221
(716) 631-2266
FAX (716) 631-2425

Products Show for Business Industry
1613 Farnham Street, Suite 666
Omaha, NE 68102-2142
(402) 346-8003
FAX (402) 346-5412

NOVEMBER SHOWS

American Marketing Assoc.
Agribusiness Conference
250 South Wacker Drive, Suite 200
Chicago, IL 60606-5819
(312) 648-0536
FAX (312) 648-9713

Great Lakes Industrial Show
33 Rutherford Avenue
Boston, MA 02129
(617) 242-6092
FAX (617) 242-1817

Industrial Expo
91-21546 Township
RD 520
Sherwood Park, AB T8E 1S5
(403) 922-5033
FAX (403) 922-5507

DECEMBER SHOWS

Expo Expo
Epic Enterprise, Inc.
8989 Rio San Diego, Suite 160
San Diego, CA 92108-1647
(619) 294-2999
FAX (619) 294-6699

International Assoc. of Fairs
Box 985
Springfield, MO 65801
(417) 862-5771
FAX (417) 862-0156

INTERNATIONAL INVENTORS' CONVENTIONS

BELGIUM

Flanders Technology International
International Jaarbeurs
Van Vlaanderen VZW
ICC Floraliaplaeis B-9000, Ghent

CANADA

Business World Exhibition
1801 McGill College Avenue, Suite 970
Montreal, Quebec H3A2N4

FRANCE

Inova
S.A. Technoexpo
8 Rue de la Michodiere
75002 Paris

GERMANY

Hannover Fair
Deutsche Messe-und Ausstellungs-AG
Messegelande
D-300 Hannover

International Exposition of Inventions
Messezentrum Nuremberg
D-8500 Nuremberg 50

JAPAN

Techno Tokyo
Promotion Division
Nihon Cogyo Jimbocho
Chiyoda-ko
Tokyo, 101

SWITZERLAND

International Exposition Inventions
Secretariat du Salon, 8
Rue du 31 Decembre
Geneva, CH-1207

EUROPEAN FAIRS AND CORRESPONDING U.S. CONTACTS

BERLIN

AMK Berlin
101 West Grand Avenue, Suite 601
Chicago, IL 60610
(312) 245-5230

DUSSELDORF

Dusseldorf Trade Shows, Inc.
Empire State Building, Suite 4621
New York, NY 10018
(212) 239-3750

FRANKFURT AND COLOGNE

German-American Chamber of Commerce, Inc.
Trade Fairs Department
666 Fifth Avenue
New York, NY 10103
(212) 974-8830

HANNOVER

Hannover Fairs USA, Inc.
P.O. Box 7066
103 Carnegie Center
Princeton, NJ 08540

MILAN
Delia Associates
Milan Fairs USA
Route 22
P.O. Box 338
West Whitehouse, NJ 08888
(201) 534-9044

MUNICH
Kallman and Associates
5 Maple Court
Ridgewood, NJ 07450
(201) 652-7070

Notes

Recommended Reading

Business Information Sources. Lorna M. Daniells. Berkeley, CA: University of California Press, 1985.

Business Services and Information: The Guide to the Federal Government. Philadelphia, PA: Management Information Exchange, 1978.

Copyright Basics. Washington, D.C.: Copyright Office, Library of Congress, 1995.

Federal Government Directory of Information Resources in the U.S. Washington, D.C.: U.S. Government Printing Office, 1994.

Finding Facts Fast: How to Find Out What You Want and Need to Know. Alden Todd. Berkeley, CA: Ten Speed Press, 1979.

Government Giveaways for Entrepreneurs II. Matthew Lesko. Kensington, MD: Information U.S.A., 1994.

Guerrilla Marketing. Jay Conrad Levinson. Boston, MA: Houghton Miffin Company, 1984.

The Guide to Venture Capital Sources. Wellesley Hills, MA: Capital Publishing.

A Handbook for Inventors. Calvin MacCrachen. New York, NY: Scribner's, 1983.

Homemade Money. Barbara Brabec. Betterway Books, 1994.

How to Cash in on Your Bright Ideas! George G. Siposs. Orange, CA: Universal Development, 1980.

The Insiders Guide to Small Business Resources. David E. Gumpert and Jeffry A. Timmons. Garden City, NY: Doubleday, 1982.

The Inventors' Handbook. Robert Park. White Hall, VA: Betterway Publications, 1990.

Inventors' Source Book. Susan Hartman and Norman Parrish. Berkeley, CA: Inventors Resource Center Publishers, 1978.

Manual of Patent Examining Procedures. Washington, D.C.: U.S. Patent and Trademark Office, 1995.

National Trade and Professional Association Directory. Washington, D.C.: Columbia Books, Inc., 1996.

New Product Development. George Gruenwald. Lincolnwood, IL: NTC Business Books, 1985.

New Product Development Strategies. Frederick Buggie. New York, NY: AMACOM, 1981.

The One Minute Manager. Kenneth Blanchard and Spencer Johnson. New York, NY: Berkley Books, 1982.

The Patent Book. James Gregory and Kevin Mulligan. New York: A&W Publishers, 1979.

Patent It Yourself. David Pressman. Berkeley, CA: Nolo Press, 1989.

Products and Markets. William H. Reynolds. New York, NY: Appleton-Century-Crofts/Meredith, 1969.

Small Business Guide to Federal R&D Funding Opportunities. Washington, D.C.: U.S. Department of Energy, Assistant General for Patents, 1995.

The Sources of Invention. John Jewkes, David Sawyers and Richard Stillerman. New York, NY: Norton, 1969.

Standard & Poor's Industry Surveys. New York, NY: Standard & Poor, Inc., 1996.

Trade Shows and Professional Exhibits Directory. Robert Elster. Detroit, MI: Gale Research Inc., 1996.

Why Did They Name It . . . ? Hannah Campbell. New York, NY: Fleet, 1964.

Why Didn't I Think of That! Robert L. Shook. New York, NY: New American Library, 1982.

Working for Yourself. Joseph Anthony. Kiplinger Books, 1995.

Working at Home. Lindsay O'Connor. Harvest, OR: Harvest Publishing, 1990.

Writing the Natural Way. Gabriele Lusser Rico. Los Angeles, CA: Tarcher, 1983.

Notes

Index

d

e

f

g

h

i

k

l

r

s

Notes

ORDER DIRECT FROM THE OASIS PRESS®

ORDER FORM

To order or for a complete catalog call toll free 1-800-228-2275

Mail or Fax to:

PSI Research / The Oasis Press
300 North Valley Drive
Grants Pass, OR 97526 USA
Inquiries and International Orders (541) 479-9464
FAX (541) 476-1479

Title	Binder	Paperback	Quantity	Cost
Export Now	☐ $39.95	☐ $24.95		
Power Marketing	☐ $39.95	☐ $19.95		
Know Your Market	☐ $39.95	☐ $19.95		
Insider's Guide to Small Business Loans	☐ $29.95	☐ $19.95		
Buyer's Guide to Business Insurance	☐ $39.95	☐ $19.95		
Marketing Mastery	☐ $39.95	☐ $19.95		
Customer Engineering	☐ $39.95	☐ $19.95		
The Business Environmental Handbook	☐ $39.95	☐ $19.95		
Successful Business Plan: Book & Software	☐ $125.95	☐ $109.95		

The software is compatible with Windows 3.1 and Windows 95!

If your purchase is:	Shipping within the USA:
$0 - $25	$5.00
$25.01 - $50	$6.00
$50.01 - $100	$7.00
$100.01 - $175	$9.00
$175.01 - $250	$13.00
$250.01 - $500	$18.00
$500.01 +	4% of total merchandise

SUBTOTAL

SHIPPING

TOTAL ORDER

International or Canadian orders, please call for a quote on shipping costs.

SOLD TO: *Please give street address.*

Name:

Title:

Company:

Street Address:

City/State/Zip:

Daytime Phone:

PAYMENT INFORMATION: *Rush service is available. Call for details.*

☐ CHECK enclosed payable to PSI Research — CHARGE ☐ VISA ☐ MASTERCARD ☐ AMEX ☐ DISCOVER

Card Number: — Expires:

Signature: — Name on Card:

REDE0497